D0266357

THE ONE SHOW BOOK OF TRUE TALES

Great British Stories of Adventure, Heroism,
Love... and the Seriously Strange

Written and compiled by Cris Warren
Contributor: Duncan Haskell

ONE PLACE. MANY STORIES

HQ
An imprint of HarperCollins*Publishers* Ltd
1 London Bridge Street
London SE1 9GF

This hardback edition 2017

2

First published in Great Britain by
HQ, an imprint of HarperCollins*Publishers* Ltd 2017

ISBN: 9780008256760

MIX
Paper from
responsible sources
FSC
www.fsc.org   **FSC™ C007454**

This book is produced from independently certified FSC paper
to ensure responsible forest management.

For more information visit: www.harpercollins.co.uk/green

Printed and bound in Great Britain by
CPI Group (UK) Ltd, Croydon, CR0 4YY

THE ONE SHOW
BOOK OF TRUE TALES

CONTENTS

CONTENTS

INTRODUCTION

Welcome to *The One Show Book of True Tales,* featuring adventure, heroism, love, loss… and the seriously strange, from the hit BBC One TV show.

In your hands is a lovingly crafted compilation of more than 100 of the quirkiest, strangest, most mind-boggling, and fascinating stories pulled from the brains of the *One Show* research desk at independent producers Icon Films. These stories were originally turned into short four-and-a-half minute films by their production teams and transmitted on *The One Show* – now celebrating ten glorious years on the telly. But we've dug a bit deeper into those mini-televisual masterpieces to bring you standalone and strangely connected tales of everyday British foibles, eccentricity, unsolved murders, very hard maths, A-list stars turning up in unexpected places, cricket-playing Nazis, epic fails, government cover-ups, mini triumphs, scientific breakthroughs and, er, even one about how a nudist film-maker came up with the object that no self-respecting hipster home could do without…

You may already be a fan of *The One Show,* but did you know that launching this now much-loved early evening weekday magazine show was a gamble for the BBC? You see, *The*

One Show sits in a tricky scheduling hinterland – 7 p.m., that awkward, sticky-out bit of time and space after the news, falling between the snoozy un-demands of daytime programmes, and before 'primetime'. This is the time of day when TV's magnetism is at its weakest for viewers; often just home from work, distracted by making, or eating, their tea, putting the bins out, wrangling toddlers toward their pyjamas, ignoring a spate of PPI compensation calls on the landline and whatever else it is people do at 7 p.m. on a weekday.

But the gamble paid off. Today *The One Show* is a colourful and quirky, serious and topical – and often a little eccentric – TV institution. Transmitting five nights a week, 46 weeks of the year, it averages five million viewers per edition; no mean feat when you consider the competition from a multi-channel TV environment and the equally distracting 'second screens' of smart phones, tablets and laptops that now accompany households when they congregate on the sofa.

Icon Films started making film shorts to be featured on *The One Show* for season one, in 2007. Originally a tiny team of two, this eventually turned into more than 20, including researchers, directors, camera ops and production managers. Together, we've produced over 500 shorts.

The demand for each film is to create 'Did you see… ?' moments – events, stunts and facts that have people talking about them the next day. These may be questions (how, exactly, would the gang in *The Italian Job* have escaped with their loot from a coach hanging precariously from an alpine cliff?); unknown stories from secret files (did you know that all the maps and cash needed for the D-Day invasions were produced and stored in a fake bakery in a Bristol suburb?); the downright bizarre (the world's first cash machine had a small man hidden inside in case it malfunctioned during its grand unveiling); or even the mysterious (in an East Midlands church yard lies the grave of an unknown man. We know how he died, we know his killer, who was hanged, but 80 years after the event, we still don't know who he is).

Once those films are commissioned, they're researched in depth; scripts are written and signed off by the BBC; onscreen contributors, locations and archives are secured; and then they're shot – usually in just one day – with one of the show's roster of star reporters. The films are edited over two days and then delivered. On average Icon Films knock out 60 of these films a year.

Making the films fit in a four-and-a-half-minute timeframe means that the stories being told have to be ground down to their bare essentials. But every single one has a plethora of fascinating extra bits that we simply couldn't fit into the films. That's the reasoning behind this book, then. Think of it as *The One Show: the Director's Cut*. It's full of facts, extended interviews and trivia nuggets drawn out from revisiting the original research and sources for the films. And we've also included a few exclusive stories too! Like the TV show that inspired it, the book is a distinctly British celebration of historic and contemporary eccentricity, innovation, bravery and sheer chutzpah – one that packs just as much water-cooler punch as its filmed equivalents featured in the show. And, like the show, if you're not completed absorbed by the story you're currently reading, we guarantee you'll love the one on the next page...

EUREKA MOMENTS

ARE YOU HAVIN' A LAVA? EDWARD CRAVEN WALKER SEES THE LIGHT

During the Second World War RAF reconnaissance pilot Edward Craven Walker flew dangerous missions over enemy territory to photograph Nazi bases. When the conflict ended, Walker continued his interest in photography: credited on-screen as Michael Keatering, he produced and occasionally appeared in naturist films, and pioneered the, admittedly niche, subgenre of nudist documentary that focused on naked, underwater, ballet. *Travelling Light* (1960) features a troupe of all-swimming, all-dancing women expressing themselves in the warm coastal waters of Corsica. British nudists, Walker's target audience, may well have been interested in the onscreen choreography, but it's unlikely many would have been inspired enough to consider following suit in British seas. Nor were they likely to be encouraged to shed their thermals by Walker's attempt to merge nakedness and winter sports with the 'documentary' *Eves On Skis* (1963).

Both films were considerable box office hits in the few UK

cinemas that screened them. In turn, further revenue was generated when they were picked up for worldwide distribution, generating enough income for Craven Walker to establish his own nudist retreat, The Bournemouth and District Outdoor Club. He became something of a spokesperson for British naturism, but he wasn't exactly egalitarian about attracting new members – especially those on the larger side. He once declared, 'We at Bournemouth have a health centre and only want healthy people here… We are against all these fat fogies – it's not what naturism should be about'.

In between all that, he invented what's popularly known as the Lava Lamp, but which Walker originally dubbed the Astro Lamp. By either name, the psychedelic beacon became shorthand for the 1960s, but it took Craven Walker most of the 1950s to develop it.

Around 1950, over a pint in the Queen's Head pub in Ringwood, Hampshire, he became mesmerised by a novelty lamp behind the bar. The lamp was invented by Donald Dunnet, a Scot living in England, but how it ended up behind the bar is a mystery. It may have been a prototype because we do know that it was patented in 1951. The lamp featured two liquids – 'one', says the patent description, 'of a lower gravity than the other, the two liquids being non-miscible and the upper layer being of lower specific gravity than the lower layer and means for heating the lower layer so that it rises through the upper layer in the form of liquid bubbles or as a liquid column which breaks into such bubbles, the bubbles being cooled by the upper layer so that they return to the lower layer.' Basically, when the liquids were heated, the lower of the two sent a column of bubbles to the top, then the light would turn off, the water cool and the bubbles sink to their original position. It was developed from one of Dunnet's earlier patents, an egg timer. This was a close-ended glass tube filled with viscous liquids that would break into bubbles after about four minutes when submerged in boiling water – time enough for the perfect boiled egg.

The bubble action fascinated Walker. He saw potential, but for what he didn't really know. Nonetheless he began tinkering with liquids and wax, heating them with a light bulb that he had installed inside an orange cordial bottle. Later he used a glass cocktail shaker – a shape that would inform the finished product. Initially this was only a hobby for Walker – he was otherwise engaged with his films and then his nudist club – but he began to devote more time to the project in the late 1950s. Finally, in 1963, he had the perfect ratio of oil and wax, and achieved a sweet-spot melting point for the wax (which continues to be produced to a secret recipe). The egg timer was now a desk light cum moving objet d'art, which he called the Astro Lamp.

The mixture of oil and wax takes several minutes to warm and become liquid but then changes form and viscosity rapidly as it rises up the water column within the tube and into the cooler water. Before it hits the bottom, the heater has melted it again and the cycle restarts. Walker created 100 different designs over the years with range of different colours.

Once on sale the hypnotic ooze created by the lamps became instant conversation pieces in the hip homes of the 1960s. They achieved cult status thanks to being featured in hit shows like *Doctor Who*, *The Avengers* and *The Prisoner*. Sales of Edward's Lava Lamp soared and even though it wasn't marketed at the cool cats of the day, its bewitching yet mellow dance was seen as an ideal accompaniment to any psychedelic trip, forever linking it with the mind-altering drugs of the time. Asked if this concerned him, Walker commented, 'If you buy my lamp, you won't need to buy drugs.' For him, the lamp was a groovy enough trip in its own right.

CASH IN A FLASH – JOHN SHEPHERD-BARRON HITS PAY-DIRT WITH THE ATM

ATM cash machines are so ubiquitous we see them only when we need them. But for weeks after the very first one went into service in 1967, people would travel from all over just to watch one magically dispense cash. It was a revolutionary concept that suddenly meant our hard-earned cash was available around the clock.

Like the Greek scientist Archimedes, who coined the phrase, the cash machine's inventor, John Shepherd-Barron, had his eureka moment in the bath in 1965.

Earlier that day he had gone to the bank, only to arrive moments after it had closed. Until as recently as the 1980s, High Street Banks kept rigid hours; if you needed cash outside of 9 a.m. to 3.30 p.m. on a weekday (9 a.m. to noon on Saturdays), you were stuck.

As he soaked, John pondered how he could liberate his money when it suited him. He hit upon the idea of a chocolate bar dispenser that instead vended cash. As an executive with bank note printers De La Rue, John was able to arrange a chat with the Chief General Manager of Barclays Bank, who gave him just 90 seconds to pitch his idea. Apparently the pitch took

85 seconds, and the bank agreed a deal: six machines initially and a contract for De La Rue to provide the armoured trucks to fill them.

John's idea wasn't too far removed from the modern machines that are now present on every high street – and the major concern was, as it is today, fraud. Plastic bankcards stored with personal information were still a way off, so Shepherd-Barron had to work out a way to ensure that the only person who could get your cash was you. He developed a two-step process for this. Step One seems positively dangerous – radioactive cheques. These were impregnated with the compound carbon-14, an isotope the machine was programmed to recognise. John played down health concerns, claiming you would have to eat over 100,000 cheques for them to have any effect on health. Step Two is much more familiar. You'd have to prove to the machine you were the right person to withdraw money by punching in a personal identification number or PIN. If that PIN corresponded with the carbon-14 numbers on the voucher, the machine would pay out.

It was John's wife Caroline who gave the world the four-digit PIN. Recalling his army days, John originally proposed using a six-digit personal identification number (PIN) but rejected the idea when Caroline insisted she could only ever remember four digits at a time. So four numbers became the world standard.

It took only two years to go from a rapid pitch to delivering the world's first cash machine. But what was the prestigious address for such a technological wonder. Tokyo? Frankfurt? New York? No, Enfield in Middlesex. By keeping the launch relatively low profile – although Reg Varney, the comedian and future star of *On the Buses,* was on hand to officially launch the machine – Barclays and partners De La Rue could play down any teething problems. In fact, being made to look foolish by the robot teller was such a concern that a smaller than average man was actually concealed inside the machine to push the first bundle of notes through the slot in case of a breakdown.

Today there are more than two million cash machines in the world, and the only real difference from the Enfield model is that we use plastic cards and not glowing cheques to access them. John Shepherd-Barron was awarded an OBE in 2004, his only real reward for the idea. Ironically, having never patented the concept because he wanted to keep carbon-14 secret from potential forgers, he didn't ever get any cash out of his own invention.

BRIGHT SPARK – WILLIAM BICKFORD INVENTS THE SAFETY FUZE

Working with gunpowder was a deadly business in the nineteenth century, so William Bickford's invention of the safety fuse – a design in use to this day – was truly life-saving. Born in Ashburton, Devon, he moved to Truro in Cornwall, where he worked as both a currier and leather merchant. Even though he had no direct involvement with the mining industry, Bickford grew increasingly troubled by the number of fatal accidents and serious injuries that resulted as miners tried to break up large masses of rock. The method at the time was to use straws or goose quills filled with gunpowder. These had a wildly unpredictable burn rate and many fatalities were caused by explosives going off before miners could reach cover or by miners walking back to see if their fuses were still burning… and discovering too late that they were.

One day in 1831 Bickford had his eureka moment while watching a friend, James Bray, twining rope. As he observed Bray twisting separate strands together, Bickford realised that a similar approach could be used in order to make a safer type of fuse. He adapted the rope-making technique by trickling gunpowder into strands of jute cord as they were being twisted together. He then coated the strands in a waterproof varnish to create the safety fuse.

To help with the process, Bickford designed a machine that would spin the strands of jute over the gunpowder for him and also prevent them from ever untwisting. The finished product was so accurate that a burn rate of 30 seconds per 1.2 m (1 ft) of fuse could be safely relied upon. All that remained was for the person laying the explosive to cut off an appropriate length, in order to guarantee a safe escape.

Bickford patented 'The Patent Safety Rod', later renamed the 'Safety Fuze', and travelled Britain's mines showing off his invention, gaining the approval of – and just as importantly, orders from – mine owners. He co-founded the factory that would eventually go on to become Bickford, Smith, & Company, and work soon began on the production of these new fuses. Within the first year, they had manufactured 72 km (45 miles) of fuse and the factory operated for more than 100 years, going on to make thousands of miles of it. Sadly, William died shortly before the factory opened and did not witness the profound effect his invention had in the mines, saving hundreds of lives and creating a process for making fuses which remains largely the same to this day. He truly was a bright spark.

STICKY BUSINESS – KINNINMONTH AND GRAY ROLL OUT SELLOTAPE

Sellotape has been generally useful for more than 80 years. Invented in 1937, in Acton, West London, it made short shrift of the wrapping of parcels – once hostage to string – and dozens of around-the-house fixes that required various pots of glues.

It's a pretty clever tool we rarely stop to appreciate. It's a simple strip of Cellophane with a rubber resin glue on one side. Developers Colin Kinninmonth and George Gray had planned to call their product Cello-Tape – because that's what it was (and is) – but Cellophane is a trademark and they were warned off.

Renamed Sellotape, it rapidly became indispensable in the home and the workplace. When the Second World War was declared, two years after Sellotape launched, it was even used for national defence.

As fears of a Blitz grew in 1938 and 1939, so rehearsals for the inevitable began – there were even test runs of blackouts in cities, which gave a taste of the casualties that could be expected in urban environments trying to function in complete darkness. But the immediate concern was the sheer amount of glass potentially flying through the air during a raid. Government issue brown tape soon criss-crossed the nation's windows – an enduring image of the plucky Home Front. The downside was it required moisture, was fiddly to apply and looked pretty ugly. Sellotape, if you could afford enough rolls, was all but invisible but, apparently, just as effective against ordnance dropped off by the Luftwaffe.

Sellotape continues to be produced in the UK, though the brand is now owned by Henkel, a German company.

STICKLERS FOR THE RULES

Like Hoover for vacuum cleaner, the British use the term Sellotape to mean any variety of sticky tape. The exception to this rule is made by the BBC children's magazine show, *Blue Peter*. During their famous 'makes' the product is referred to as 'sticky tape' so as not to contravene BBC rules about advertising. This is admirable, of course, but past presenters have been known to refer to 'sticky back plastic', which is misleading. 'Sticky back plastic' refers to cut-to-size sheets of, usually patterned, Cellophane, one side of which has to be peeled off to activate the adhesive. This is the kind of information that wins pub quizzes and one day you'll thank us for including it.

BELT UP! BUILDER OF WORLD'S FIRST GLIDER ENCOURAGES SERVANT TO CRASH IT

It's one of the most important inventions of modern times, but the first man to wear a seatbelt didn't really appreciate it at the time.

In the mid-nineteenth century, John Appleby was a coachman for the 'father of aviation' Sir George Cayley. His employer had created a full-sized glider, an aircraft that has no engine but which uses currents of air for flight. As Appleby was about to find out, this would be the world's first successful glider – complete with a strap device to hold the pilot into the seat.

Appleby's contribution to aviation cannot be underestimated. He set in stone the aerodynamic forces of flight – weight, lift, drag and thrust – and he dreamt up cambered wings, the fundamental of aircraft design. All of this was about to be put to the test when Cayley's glider was prepared to take its maiden flight.

But Sir George, then aged 80, was neither light enough nor nimble enough to sit in the driving seat of such a contraption himself, so Appleby was volunteered. Technically Appleby might not have been the first person in the world to fly a glider (if you count probably hundreds of prior attempts), but he *was* the world's first wearer of a seatbelt. Just as well. The glider flew 183 m (600 ft) and crash-landed. John reportedly screamed, 'Sir George, I wish to give notice. I was hired to drive, not to fly.'

Though the seatbelt was later patented for use in cars in the USA in 1885 by New Yorker Edward J. Claghorn, Sir George remains credited as the inventor, and he campaigned to see seatbelts fitted into trains.

On 31 January 1983, it became a legal requirement to wear seatbelts in cars on UK roads.

LOUIS LE PRINCE – KING OF CINEMA

Number One Dock Street in Leeds, a Victorian office and warehouse that's been converted into luxury apartments, can make a valid claim to being the birthplace of the motion picture.

In 1888, from the window on the third floor, French

photographer and inventor Louis Le Prince hand-cranked photographic paper through a camera he had designed and built himself to capture the street scene below. The resulting clip, two seconds long and shot at 20 frames per second, showed horse-drawn carriages and pedestrians crossing Leeds Bridge in almost 'real' time. In spite of its brevity, this snippet of life 130 years ago is the most important documentary ever made – the world's first successful moving picture.

The story of how this defining moment came about begins in France in 1842, when Le Prince was born. As a child, he often visited the studio of his father's friend Louis Daguerre, who was one of the pioneers of photography.

He moved to Leeds in 1866 after being invited to join a family firm of brass founders by John Whitely, a college friend. He then married John's sister Elizabeth, who was a talented artist. Together they established a school of applied art, and became renowned for their photography work. It was here that he saw Eadweard Muybridge's pictures of a galloping horse – taken with a series of 12 still cameras set up along a route and then animated to look like motion. Although Muybridge had succeeded in portraying a galloping horse in a photographic sequence using multiple stills, this was not an economical, practical or easy way of creating moving images. Le Prince wanted to go one step further and capture moving images on a single camera.

Le Prince's first film camera was partly inspired by Muybridge's multiple-camera setup. It featured 16 lenses, and each took one photograph, fractions of a second apart. Although the camera was capable of 'capturing' motion, this wasn't a complete success because each lens photographed the subject from a slightly different viewpoint, meaning that the projected image jumped about.

Then came Louis' eureka moment. He realised that he needed to use one lens and capture multiple images on a single strip of paper, to avoid the laborious task of stitching the still images together. By turning a handle, Le Prince was able to spool a roll of photographic paper past a rotating shutter. However, in order to capture a steady, non-blurred image, he had to invent a clamping and releasing mechanism that would ensure the paper held steady for the fraction of time it needed to be correctly exposed. His first attempts managed to capture 12 frames per second – not enough to portray smooth, real-looking motion. Remodelling the camera to shoot 20 frames per second, he lugged it up three flights of stairs in Dock Street and positioned it at the window. He deliberately chose the location, knowing it to be one of the busiest spots in Leeds, and started to turn the crank. The rest is…

Well, actually, it isn't. In spite of his remarkable achievement, Le Prince is anything but a household name. He'd ploughed all of his money into developing his camera, and applying for UK and European patents was proving to be a complicated logistical and bureaucratic challenge. There was an enormous amount of interest in his work – especially from agents of the Edison Company in the USA. That may have spurred Le Prince into arranging to travel to America to demonstrate his camera and get a US patent before anyone else could. But first he needed to pay a quick visit to the continent, to see his architect brother in France – in order to claim his share of an inheritance. Not only did he fail to stake his claim but the trip also seems to have cost him his life. On 16 September 1890,

Louis Le Prince boarded a train at Dijon, bound for Paris. He never arrived. Louis and his luggage – among it his precious camera – seemed to have disappeared into thin air.

Le Prince's body was never found. As there was no proof that he had died, his family couldn't protect his inventions. A year later, Edison successfully patented his own motion picture camera. Le Prince's family was distraught and entered into a long copyright legal battle, even accusing Edison of having Le Prince murdered. It's an accusation that has never been proved.

IN LIVING COLOUR

Despite being nicknamed 'Daftie' as a child, Edinburgh-born James Clerk Maxwell went on to become one of the great nineteenth-century scientists. From his colour vision studies, Maxwell found that all the colours of nature could be counterfeited to the eye by mixing just three pure colours of light – red, green and blue. In May 1861 he presented the first-ever colour photograph at a lecture he gave to the Royal Institute.

His pioneering demonstration used an image of a tartan ribbon photographed three times. A trio of exposures of the ribbon were taken through red, green and blue filters and then projected through separate magic lanterns in order to create one single image – the first colour photo. These experiments have formed the basis of nearly all photochemical and electronic colour photography since.

COLD CASES TO HEAT UP YOUR INNER DETECTIVE

THE GRAVE OF THE UNKNOWN MAN

As a travelling lingerie salesman with an eye for the ladies, Alfred Rouse had a suitcase stuffed with secrets. But the pressure of multiple lives was mounting, and the only way out, he reasoned, was the perfect murder. His own.

Alfred Rouse had served with distinction on the battlefields of the First World War, but a serious head wound caused by an exploded shell left him, according to his doctors, 'easily excited... (he) laughs immoderately at times.' He had another strange affliction – an inability to stop talking.

Back in civvies, Alfred appeared to be highly respectable. But his transient job, as well as the gift of the gab and a roving eye, resulted in a bigamous marriage, a string of lovers across the UK and at least two illegitimate children.

Rouse's finances and sanity were taking a bruising. Chased

by paternity suits and attempting to keep his multiple lovers happy, he became increasingly desperate to put a lid on things and on Guy Fawkes Night in 1931 he executed what he thought was a perfect plan to start his life over. Everybody would think he'd been killed in a car crash.

To fake his own death, he decided that somebody had to die to take his place. The case files are held at Northamptonshire Police Headquarters and make eye-popping reading to this day. Police archivist Richard Cowley explains: 'Rouse met a man in a London pub who was a similar build to him and the idea formed that he would be his victim. On the afternoon of the 5th of November, Rouse duped the man to get into the car and Rouse and the man drove north.' With Bonfire Night as a cover, Rouse was planning his own blaze. 'Pulling into a quiet Northampton street, he pounced.' Rouse knocked his victim unconscious before 'dousing the body in petrol; he lit a match and ran for cover.'

But Rouse's inability to keep shtum placed him at the scene.

At 2 a.m. on 6 November 1930, two young men walking home from a party came across the blazing Morris car. From behind a hedge a man popped out, chuckled and jauntily commented: 'It looks as if someone's had a bonfire,' before strolling off.

When the scene was investigated, the police discovered a body, burnt beyond recognition. The number plates were traced to an Albert Rouse and it was presumed the charred remains were his. But then the two young men came forward to tell of their encounter. Northamptonshire Police became suspicious and an identikit based on the description of the 'chatty man' was circulated.

Rouse was spotted in London and arrested as he got off a bus. Under interrogation, Rouse said he'd picked up the hitch-hiker, who had never revealed his name and who was drunk. Alfred stopped the car to relieve himself by the roadside. He asked the hitchhiker to fill the car up with petrol from a jerry can. The hitchhiker, who was puffing away on a cigar given to him by Rouse, spilt petrol over himself and then dropped the cigar. Rouse said he tried to save him, to no avail. Then he panicked and ran away.

Rouse might well have got away with a charge of accidental death but he just couldn't stop talking. He revealed to incredulous police officers details about his numerous lovers (referring to them as 'my harem', which particularly annoyed one of the detectives), and moaned about the demands for the upkeep of his legion of children. The police decided to charge him with murder.

Rouse's alibi was systematically destroyed in court. It was almost immediately established that Alfred didn't smoke, so his cigar story was stubbed out. Bernard Spilsbury, the pioneer of forensic investigation, also proved that Rouse had killed his victim with a mallet (not, as Rouse claimed, strangulation) before setting fire to him. Forensics also proved that Rouse had modified the car so that the fire would be accelerated.

The trial lasted six days and the jury took just 25 minutes to decide that Rouse was guilty. Rouse was sentenced to be hanged at Bedford Gaol on 10 March 1931. As he waited in his cell for the hangman, Tom Pierrepoint, to place a noose around his neck, Rouse filled the time by writing a long letter to the *Daily Sketch* newspaper. He confirmed the findings of the prosecution and detailed how he murdered his victim.

One key question remained: who was that innocent victim tragically caught up in Rouse's bizarre scheme? His remains were buried in the graveyard of St Edmund's Church, Hardingstone, Northampton. The grave is simply inscribed: 'In Memory of an Unknown Man'. Rouse said in his letter to the press that his victim was chosen because he was precisely 'the sort of man nobody would miss'.

But William Briggs, who went missing in 1930, was sorely missed and the event haunted his family for generations to come. Briggs was just 23 when he left the family home for an appointment and never returned. His surviving family long believed that William may have been Rouse's unfortunate victim. William's niece Jean has spent her life wondering what happened to her mother's brother. 'It's all the things I've heard as a child that my mother has told me about. We've never known and I know she was so upset and wanted to find out. So I would like to find out for her.' William's great-grandniece, Samantha, says there was circumstantial evidence that shouldn't be discounted:

A lot of the family stories we've got, such as William leaving the family home dressed in a plum suit – well, there was plum cloth found at the scene of the crime. William also had auburn hair and a sample of auburn hair was found. There are a lot of things in the crime report that match the stories we've grown up with.

The family approached Dr John Bond, a forensic scientist at the University of Leicester (where DNA fingerprinting was pioneered), who specialises in investigating cold cases. 'Initially

I thought that probably after all this time it's very unlikely we'll be able to do anything to help,' he says. But tissue samples had been taken from the victim during the autopsy and then subsequently filed away and forgotten. 'That was sort of a Eureka moment and I thought, yes, maybe we can get some DNA from this to try and help the family.'

However, there was no DNA match to link Jean to the victim. Jean expressed relief that it wasn't William who met such a gruesome end but frustration that, so far, there is no closure for either her family or that of the unknown man.

WHO'S QUALTROUGH?

On 20 January 1931, housewife Julia Wallace was brutally murdered in her home in Liverpool. Three months later, her husband William Wallace was convicted of the murder and faced the death penalty – only to make legal history when his conviction was overturned by the Court of Appeal.

W. H. Wallace was a highly respected and respectable insurance agent, the archetypical 'Man from the Pru' whose hobby was playing chess; he was rumoured to be a Grandmaster. His wife Julia was equally 'proper', and their neighbours in Liverpool believed they were the very picture of happiness.

One night at his chess club, Wallace received a message that a man named Qualtrough had called, asking Wallace to visit his home on a 'matter of business', 6 km (4 miles) away at 25 Menlove Gardens East, Mossley Hill. Wallace had never heard of Qualtrough, but presuming the address was near Menlove Avenue, where he had clients, he travelled to the location – only to discover that no such man and no such place existed. When he got home, later that night, Wallace discovered his wife dead in the parlour. She had been bludgeoned.

The Julia Wallace case was the real-life whodunit that captured imaginations in the Britain of the 1930s. To this day it has never been solved. But after years of painstaking research one man thinks he may have finally solved the case.

John Gannon, a crime writer from Liverpool who wrote the book *The Killing of Julia Wallace,* was the first person to be given access to the files of both Merseyside Police and William Wallace's solicitor, Hector Munro. He says:

> At the time of the investigation the police identified that the anonymous caller had used a telephone box only 400 yards away from the Wallace's home. The police became convinced that the whole thing had been an elaborate plan by Wallace to murder his wife. She was last seen alive ten minutes before his alleged departure time by a milk boy making his rounds. They thought that he could have killed his wife and still have had time to make the journey to Menlove.

The judge, however, disagreed and instructed the jury to move for an acquittal. But the jury had been swayed by the police's version of events. Wallace was sentenced to death by hanging. Less than two weeks later, the appeal judges quashed the verdict on the grounds that the prosecution had not proved their case sufficiently.

So if it wasn't Wallace, who was it? During his interrogation Wallace told the police about one man who might have been responsible for his wife's murder. That man was called Gordon Parry. John explains, 'Parry had worked briefly for

Wallace before he was fired. He also had a criminal record, and knew where Wallace kept his insurance takings. During the murder £4 [approximately £240 today] had been stolen, according to Wallace. Parry was heavily in debt, and may have held a grudge towards Wallace.' There was one final piece of evidence pointing towards Parry. At the time of the murder a young mechanic named John Parkes had seen Parry arrive at his garage and wash his car down. 'Parkes saw a glove in the car and realised it was wet with blood.'

Wallace's 11-hour acquittal at Liverpool Crown Court marked a turning point in the British legal system, says criminologist Barry Godfrey.

> The King vs Wallace was arguably one of the most important cases in recent British legal history. It marked the transition from a Victorian legal and moral framework to that of an enlightened, modern, evidence-based one. The judiciary was for the first time saying that even if a jury convicts someone, if there is insufficient evidence to prove beyond reasonable doubt that they are guilty, then a jury's verdict can be overturned.

Such an important precedent was set because the jury had condemned Wallace on the police's belief that he was guilty, not on actual evidence. 'By overturning the verdict the judiciary was proving that the legal system works, that a man is innocent until *proven* guilty,' says Barry.

But whilst legal history had been made, Julia Wallace's killer was as anonymous as ever. Perhaps it was Gordon Parry. It could still even have been Wallace. Or perhaps, as John Gannon believes, there was a third man.

William Wallace had found out that he had a terminal illness and had only a few years to live. Wallace had had a kidney removed surgically and his remaining kidney was starting to fail – as was his marriage. Gannon suspects that as a result of his illness Wallace was now impotent and Julia Wallace was paying men for sex. William even discovered an amount of cash hidden in Julia's corsets – the equivalent of £70 in today's money – and that Wallace's younger colleague at 'The Pru', Joseph Marsdon, was a regular visitor to the Wallace household. Could Wallace have been inspired by this set of circumstances to plan the perfect way to get rid of Julia? John explains:

> Wallace knew that Marsdon was broke, but he was also set to marry into a wealthy family. Wallace threatened Marsdon, cleverly. He said he was going to divorce Julia on the grounds of her affair with Marsdon. That would drag Marsdon's name through the divorce courts and ruin his chances of marrying into money. Marsdon had no choice but to commit the murder on Wallace's behalf.

But there's still the issue of the phone call from the strange Mr Qualtrough. 'That,' suggests John, 'was a simple matter of bribing the destitute and unwitting Gordon Parry to make the phone call, leaving Wallace himself free to create his alibi while looking for the fictional Qualtrough.' All this whilst Marsdon committed the murder.

The Julia Wallace case has been described as an example of the perfect murder. Now, more than 80 years later, there is a third possible version of events. Has John Gannon solved the killing that changed legal history? The verdict is up to you, the jury. However, don't forget what happened when it was up to the original jury.

Wallace returned to his Liverpool home after being released. But local rumours about his guilt dogged him and he moved to the suburbs of the city. He died two years later, aged 54. No one has been charged with Julia's murder and as there is no statute of limitations for murder the case is still open, albeit very cold.

THE BOOK OF JOHN HORWOOD

John Horwood was convicted and executed for the murder of Eliza Balsom in 1821, but the case was on shaky ground from the start.

Horwood, from Hanham near Bristol, had been romantically pursuing Balsom, from Kingswood, also near Bristol, for some months. Seeing her one day with another young man, Horwood threw a stone at her in frustration.

She was bruised by the incident but otherwise, it seemed, unharmed. Two days later, and after walking some four miles from Kingswood to the centre of the city, she reported to the Bristol Infirmary feeling unsteady on her feet. She was treated for a head wound but died within days. A surgeon, Richard Smith, inspected her body and found an abscess. The fact that this was more likely to have been from an infection such as sepsis, caused by a dirty bandage applied in the hospital, was not considered, and Horwood was arrested and charged with her murder.

Horwood was hanged at a massively attended public execution outside the gates of the City's New Gaol. The moment he was pronounced dead, his body was commandeered by Richard Smith. Smith dissected the body during a public medical lecture.

Smith subsequently had Horwood's body skinned and tanned. After it was given a further chemical treatment in Bedminster, what was left of Horwood was dispatched to a bookbinder in Essex, who used it to bind a book written by Smith about the Horwood case. (This practice, known as anthropodermic bibliopegy, wasn't wholly uncommon at the time.) The book remains in the city archive and the gruesome tome is made available to the public by appointment.

Horwood's skeleton was retained by the clearly obsessed Smith, who kept it at home. It was bequeathed to Bristol Royal Infirmary and later given to Bristol University, who kept it in a cupboard. John's fate was made all the more undignified by the fact that the noose that hanged him was kept in place around his neck. In 2011 John Horwood's skeleton was released to his surviving family and he was finally buried, next to his father, at Christchurch in his hometown of Hanham.

DID FABIAN SACRIFICE THE TRUTH FOR A CRACKING YARN?

In 1954 the BBC broadcast a revolutionary new crime drama called *Fabian of the Yard*. It was based on the real-life investigations of legendary detective Robert Fabian. Fabian himself topped and tailed the show with a short piece to camera. This was a trope used in another, later, TV police institution called *Dixon of Dock Green*, but *Fabian of the Yard*'s storylines were based on real cases that he'd (usually) solved to see justice served. Fabian was most famous living and fictional detective of the age rolled into one.

He was a character on and off screen, famous for his thoroughness and his tenacity – and for embracing the new techniques of forensic science. Fabian was also aware of his own legend and rarely passed up a publicity opportunity, especially after he retired from the force and had memoirs to sell. That said, he was decorated for heroism and he was genuinely respected by his colleagues in the force as well as by his foes in the underworld.

But there was one case that he would never crack and which would haunt him for years to come. It's a tale of murder and witchcraft set in the sleepy village of Lower Quinton in Warwickshire.

It began on Valentine's Day, 1945. In a field near Meon Hill, a prehistoric hill fort in sight of Lower Quinton, lay the lifeless body of a 74-year-old man. He was pinioned to the ground with a pitchfork and had been slashed to death with a billhook, a type of hand-held scythe. Later reports state that a cross was carved into the chest, but there is no mention of this in the original autopsy.

That unofficial detail – after no less than an official pathologist's report, by the way – should be treated as the first of many alarm bells. It's characteristic of how the case has been 'remembered' and mutated; ancient myths, contemporary facts and local hearsay have meshed over the years into a horror tale worthy of the Hammer treatment. And Fabian's account of things, in his entertaining 1950 memoir *Fabian of The Yard* from which this story quotes, should be taken with a pinch of salt. After all, he failed to crack the case, so blaming a supernatural element is a pretty convenient get-out clause.

The victim's name was Charles Walton, a septuagenarian farmhand and the village loner. In life he wasn't fondly regarded. In death his macabre murder made headlines, and Warwickshire police asked Scotland Yard for assistance. The Yard dispatched their best man, Fabian, hoping that his advanced crime fighting techniques would crack the case.

'Walton had lived in the area all his life and shared this cottage with his niece, Edie. There were quite a few people who believed he practised witchcraft and that he kept natterjack toads as familiars,' says local historian Dave Matthews. (Familiars are pets owned by witches and warlocks, and commanded to do their bidding.) Dave continues:

> On the night of his murder, two eyewitnesses saw him pass through the churchyard and on up to Hillground field on the slopes of Meon Hill. He'd been working for Alfred Potter of Firs farm and Potter reported seeing him at midday repairing the hedgerows. The alarm was first raised at 6 p.m., when Walton failed to return home. Just after nightfall Edie Walton, Alfred Potter and a friend went looking for him and found him dead a short distance from the field.

The local constabulary was called to the murder scene. The Metropolitan Police report of the investigation – MEPO 3/2290, held in the National Archives at Kew – records that the first police officer at the scene was PC Michael James Lomasney. 'He arrived at 7.05 p.m. Detectives of Stratford-upon-Avon CID arrived later in the evening and Professor James M. Webster, of the West Midlands Forensic Laboratory, arrived at 11.30 p.m. The body was removed at 1.30 a.m.'

Locally, the gruesome murder and the way it had been executed sparked rumours of ritual sacrifice. Some recounted to the almost salivating tabloid reporters the tale of Ann Tennant who, 70 years earlier, had been accused of being a witch and was murdered with a pitchfork near to where Walton was found.

Others cited another report, from the late nineteenth century, about a young boy from the village, whose name just also happened to be Charles Walton. He had encountered a giant black dog on Meon Hill and then returned home to discover his sister had died. (Black dogs in English folklore are a portent of death – *The Hound of the Baskevilles*, published in 1902, takes its cue from that belief.)

In fact, Ann Tennant was murdered in front of witnesses by a certifiable lunatic – there was nothing ritualistic about it. And there is no evidence linking the Charles Walton of 1885 to the murdered Charles Walton.

When Fabian arrived, he immediately focused on the fact that Walton's tin watch and his money belt were missing. Walton always kept both items about his person, so robbery seemed a good motive – and finding that watch could be key to finding the murderer. But Fabian didn't discount witchcraft as a second line of enquiry.

By mid-afternoon the next day, Detective Inspector Fabian had brought the twentieth century to the village of Lower Quinton. An RAF surveillance plane shot across the countryside, providing high-resolution photographs of the surrounding area. The image was so detailed it even picked out the bloodstains and the trampled grass. Fabian's detectives began to plot the movements over the previous 24 hours of every last resident in the surrounding area.

But this was where cutting-edge technology was brought to its knees by a village determined to keep a secret.

By the end of the week Fabian had interviewed all 493 villagers. He was troubled by their reluctance to talk about anything other than the failure of that year's harvest. There were whispers that Walton, a bitter piece of work with no love for his fellow villagers, was to blame for this; that he had let his natterjack toad familiars hop through the fields to blast (ie destroy) the crops. Accordingly, his blood was spilt by the murderer, or even murderers, in order to bring the land back to fertility.

Fabian wrote, 'The natives of Lower Quinton are of a secretive disposition and do not take easily to strangers... Many could not make eye contact and some even became physically ill after questioning.'

On another occasion, he wrote, he and his team were met by a collective silence when they entered the local pub.

Seventy years later, people are still talking about why Fabian was stonewalled by the entire village. Graham Saunders is a former police officer, who grew up in Lower Quinton, and Fabian's arrival and investigation is still a vivid childhood memory. 'I remember groups of men going from house to house in the village with clipboards, wearing long dark overcoats and trilby hats.' Graham believes the village stayed quiet because '. . . Quinton people are very proud and they didn't like to think that this could happen in the village and I think that is the reason why they just shut up. After they had left, no one talked about the murder while I was growing up at all.'

Graham's own instinct is that the murder was committed by an outsider:

You have to remember that this was during the war. Enemy paratroopers had been popping up all over the countryside and there were POW camps in the area. Back then villagers had good cause to be wary of strangers. And as for the wall of silence, it's likely that no one knew anything about the murder. I don't think it was a cover-up. It was splashed across all the papers and was a disgrace to Lower Quinton. That's why everyone is keen to forget the story.

The ritual aspect Walton's murder is a good story, but as Graham points out, it's *not* the story.

They were a superstitious bunch back then. I once brought back a snake in a bucket with some friends and my grand-mother was horrified that it would affect the fertility of the crops. Such old wives' tales must have seemed absurd to Fabian and his men from the city. But there was never any proof at all to substantiate any of the bizarre rumours which have persisted over the years. The most likely motive was robbery. There was talk of Walton receiving £300 that month from gambling, which was completely illegal in those days, so it was a practice which attracted a dangerous crowd. Fabian strongly suspected Alfred Potter, Walton's employer, for con-taminating the murder scene and leaving his fingerprints on the murder weapon, but this was purely speculation. I doubt we'll ever find out the truth.

In the end Fabian took 4,000 statements and traced gypsies, tinkers and tramps who had passed through the village. But the murderer was never found. In his final interview, one suspect replied, 'He's been dead and buried a month now, what are you worried about?'

The land surrounding Lower Quinton has long been home to sacred sites and stone circles, but one stone that no longer stands is Walton's gravestone. It disappeared from the church-yard, removed by an upset relative who was fed up with the media interest.

To this day Charles Walton's murder remains the oldest unsolved crime in Warwickshire Police history. Fabian remained convinced that the village knew the answer and was guarding a secret.

In his report on the case, there is no mention of witchcraft as an official, or indeed any, line of enquiry. His memoir suggests he believed – at least for literary effect – otherwise. He wrote:

> I advise anybody who is tempted at any time to venture into Black Magic, witchcraft, Shamanism – call it what you will – to remember Charles Walton and to think of his death, which was clearly the ghastly climax of a pagan rite. There is no stronger argument for keeping as far away as possible from the villains with their swords, incense and mumbo-jumbo. It is prudence on which your future peace of mind and even your life could depend.

There is a weird coda to Fabian's telling of the case. Preparing to leave Lower Quinton, he took a last walk around the village and surrounding fields. At the foot of Meon Hill he was nearly knocked off his feet by a large black dog that appeared as if from nowhere and came haring across the grass directly towards him. Seconds later a small boy came down the same hill. 'Was that your dog?' asked the stunned detective. 'What dog?' the boy replied.

Of the actual case, Fabian signed off his memoirs with the following: 'Maybe one day, someone will talk, but not to me, a stranger from London. But in the office of the Warwickshire Constabulary, I happen to know, this case is not yet closed.'

EPIC FAILS

DON'T TELL HIM, PIKE!

Cliff Twemlow may not be a household name but, to fans of the more esoteric end of the cult entertainment spectrum in the early 1970s and beyond, he is a giant of stage, screen, incidental music, literature – and bodybuilding. Indeed, to many in his hometown of Manchester he's a legend who sits comfortably on the same pedestal as that city's great actors, writers and musicians.

Cliff was a showman with huge enthusiasm for all his artistic endeavours. He was, in turn, a nightclub bouncer, music composer, stuntman, actor, pulp fiction writer and director. He ran a dinosaur-themed visitor attraction and was also rumoured to be great mates with superstar Richard Gere. As an artiste, Cliff had plenty of on- and off-screen credits: as an actor he lit up a number of straight-to-VHS films, including *The Eye of Satan* and *Lethal Impact*; and as a composer his lilting melodies added a touch of class to soft-core porn flicks like *Mary Millington's True Blue Confessions*.

In 1982 Cliff decided it was time to bring together all his

talents in one fabulous, blockbusting package. Inspired by the Steven Spielberg-directed film *Jaws* – where the small American community of Amity is terrorised by a 7.6 m (25 ft) long, man-eating shark – he proposed to go full auteur by writing, directing, casting, composing and even acting in a watery horror in which a small community located at Lake Windermere (in the Lake District) is terrorised by a 3.6 m (12 ft) long, man-eating... pike.

The ambitious film would require a budget far in excess of the peanuts that funded the type of films with which Cliff was more usually associated. One way of raising that, he reasoned, would be to plant the idea in the psyche of the nation. So he set out to convince people that the scenario faced by the protagonists of his screenplay could really happen – to anyone.

Cliff needed to do for the reputation of the lowly pike what *Jaws* author Peter Benchley had done for sharks. Generally speaking, pike grow to a maximum of 1.5 m (5 ft). Of course, it would be unpleasant to be at the wrong end of such an angry pike... if you're a smaller fish. Most humans, though, will survive the rare nip on the big toe meted out by a pike if disturbed. But Cliff wasn't going to let facts get in the way of a good idea. Asked in a local TV interview if his story was backed, even loosely, by evidence, he replied: '... the largest pike ever caught was 19 ft [5.7 m]. And pike can be dangerous, you know, there's no two ways about it.'

As an aside, it's worth noting that the worldwide success of *Jaws* served, in many ways, only to justify the wholesale destruction of all species of sharks. Benchley was horrified that his pulp thriller had such ramifications and became a vocal advocate of shark conservation. But with the best, or worst, will in the world, Cliff's film was unlikely to impact pike stocks in any meaningful way.

The monster fish central to the film needed to be nothing short of awe-inspiring. Size mattered. Cliff needed to get the industry talking and investors opening their wallets, so he commissioned artist Charles Wyatt and submarine manufacturer George Coloquhoun (pronounced Ku-Hoon, by the way) to create two 3.6 m (12 ft) long pike models that had snapping, bone-smashing jaws and which could actually swim. Charles, who'd met Cliff by chance in a gym, recalls that 'he commissioned me to make a sculpture of a painting of a huge pike I'd done. I didn't really know what I was doing!' George, meanwhile, was in charge of bringing the beasts to life. 'We actually caught some pike and put them in a swimming pool so we could study how the fish moved.'

George's submarine engineering skills resulted in two, fierce-looking model pike – one that was powered by an internal engine. 'It was cutting-edge technology,' says George. The BBC science show *Tomorrow's World* agreed and ran a piece about the precursor to animatronics created in a shed in Cumbria.

As George and Charles sweated it out in the workshops, Cliff called a press conference to unveil the beast and announce a triumphant piece of casting: Joan Collins. This was quite something; La Collins was heading the *Dynasty* cast as the extremely glamorous vamp Alexis Carrington and the show, reaching the end of its first season, was a huge hit. Career-wise, going from the rarefied, sequined shoulder-padded world of Colorado oligarchs to being menaced by a fish in the Lake District either showed Joan's commitment to not being typecast – or, more likely, a very generous fee. Whatever her motivation,

Joan came to the shores of Lake Windermere to meet the press and show her support for the film.

Fixing an actorly gaze down at the cameras she said, 'What is under the water has always been very, very frightening, sort of nightmarish... and people like to be scared.'

Andrew Wilson was a reporter for the local paper, the *Lakeland Echo*, when the media circus came to town: 'Somebody rang me, I think from the hotel, and said "Joan is actually here." She certainly performed brilliantly...'

The same, unfortunately, cannot be said of the pike, which refused to work on any level the moment it was placed in the water. Sensing disaster – and a good photo opportunity – Joan Collins spontaneously put her head inside the toothy jaws of the pike and gurned, glamorously, for the snappers.

It wasn't enough to save the film, sadly. A non-functioning fish was a huge turn-off for investors and the project was, well, dead in the water.

Undoubtedly *The Pike* was a disaster and significant setback, yet it feels churlish to call it a failure since Cliff Tremlow's entire purpose seemed to be to pack his life with as much incident, enthusiasm, creativity and fun as possible. The final line of his autobiography, *Tuxedo Warrior*, declares that 'it is far better to be a resident on the brink of hell, than spend a lifetime in a relentless pursuit of a mythical heaven.' The philosophy of an epic winner, surely.

BRITISH B-MONSTERS

Had *The Pike* been made, would it have been as fêted as *Jaws*, the film it was inspired by? Likely it would have been ridiculed in the newspapers that could be bothered to review it and then forgotten, like the following selection of British B-movies that were actually made. *Trog* (1970) is the story of an ape-man living in the Home Counties, and a film so spectacularly stupid it features a scene in which the hairy beast dances to easy-listening jazz. *Gorgo* (1961) is a thinly veiled *Godzilla* rip-off about a giant reptile that terrorises London, and was made for about a quarter of the budget of the Chewits advert. Then there's 1954's *Devil Girl from Mars*, the salacious story of a Martian she-devil and her robot sidekick rounding up the male inhabitants of a small Scottish village for a breeding programme. And who could forget *Konga* (aka *I Was a Teenage Gorilla*, 1961), the tale of a botanist's botched experiment on a chimpanzee. Why would a plant scientist carry out experiments on primates? You'll have to watch the film for the explanation. Although, even then, trust me, it still won't make any sense. The results of the experiment see London (or Croydon, to be precise) being laid to waste by a stuntman in a gorilla suit. By comparison, *The Pike* looks like a sane investment opportunity.

TWANG!! FAILS TO HIT TARGET

In 1960, Lionel Bart forever changed the face of British musical theatre history. *Oliver!*, his West End adaptation of Charles Dickens' iconic novel *Oliver Twist*, took the capital by storm, before finding equal success across the pond on Broadway. It was a massive achievement in every sense, not least because Bart couldn't read or write music. Instead he came up with the melodies and lyrics in his head and then hummed them to a transcriber.

With that glittering success under his belt, Bart turned his substantial talents to another classic figure of British literature: Robin Hood. The resulting musical, *Twang!!*, was a burlesque parody of the fabled outlaw and his merry men, featuring silly disguises, a 'court tart' and a Scottish villain by the name of Roger the Ugly.

Based on the success of *Oliver!*, the biggest names in British comedy, including Ronnie Corbett, Bernard Bresslaw and Barbara Windsor, were itching to don green tights. What could possibly go wrong?

Much, is the answer. Bart, an erratic figure at the best of times, was enjoying his newfound celebrity. He was drinking heavily and experimenting with psychedelic drugs, which may explain some of *Twang!!*'s absurd plotlines. The director was Joan Littlewood, a hugely influential figure in British theatre who had triumphed earlier that decade with *Oh, What a Lovely War!*, but a disastrous preview in Manchester in November 1965 led to her jumping ship. Last-minute script changes only served to confuse matters more, and the show opened in disarray at London's Shaftesbury Theatre on 20 December 1965.

At the 11th hour, Bart decided the play needed to be camper, and threw some transvestism into the mix for good measure. The conductor fainted, an electrical fault meant the house lights kept coming on and bickering actors and stagehands could be heard throughout. It was, by all accounts, an unmitigated and epic fail. The show closed within weeks, costing Bart his personal fortune and leading eventually to his bankruptcy.

IT'S NOT THE REAL THING

Coca-Cola is the best-selling soft drink in the world, and the world's biggest soft drinks company, so how did they make what some industry experts reckon was one of the biggest marketing cockups of all time?

Instantly recognisable, Coca-Cola had triumphed thanks to slick marketing creating one of the most successful companies in the world, with a back catalogue of expensive and highly produced advertising campaigns. But the biggest marketing arsenal in the world is no defence when public tastes change. In the late 1990s Coke sales had begun to plateau as consumers turned their attention to healthier alternatives, like bottled water.

In 1999 Coke launched their own bottled water brand called Dasani. They'd been pipped to the post some five years earlier by their number one rival PepsiCo, whose bottled water brand was called Aquafina. But Dasani quickly became the second most popular brand of water in the USA. Coke looked to Europe and the UK, certain they could repeat the success. Britain alone presented a very tempting market to dive into

– sales of bottled water here had grown by nearly 50 per cent between 2000 and 2004.

So it was that in February 2004 Coke's waters broke in the UK. Dasani, baptised with a £7 million marketing splash, steamed onto the supermarket shelves.

But one man was about to muddy the waters.

In 2004 Graham Hiscott, now business editor at the *Daily Mirror*, was a journalist for the Associated Press news agency. He was leafing through *The Grocer* – the venerable magazine of the food and drink industry – and came across an article about the launch of Dasani. It was a straightforward piece, but one sentence leapt out, describing Dasani as 'mineral enhanced... tap water'. Graham could taste a story.

The perception of mineral water in the UK and Europe is that it's drawn from a remote natural spring or a bubbling mountainside brook – not, as the Dasani story revealed, a tap in a depot in the southeast London suburb of Sidcup. Coke never made explicit claims that their water had been pumped from a mountain stream by cherubs and fairies – but their constant claims of its being purer-than-pure suggested some effort had gone to source it.

The natural, honest-to-goodness image of Dasani was sullied. And then someone worked out Coke's profit margin. Dasani sold for 95p per bottle, each only 500ml (17fl oz). Thames Water, the original source of the contents via a tap, charged (at the time) 0.03p per 500ml. That's a markup of more than 3,000 per cent. To the untrained, un-business, savvy eye of the consumer, it looked as if Coke were taking the p***. Fate, of course, then arranged for swathes of Surbiton to be flooded by a burst water main, the very same water main supplying the Dasani plant.

Consumers felt let down by a household brand name, and that ensured the story ran and ran. 'It was only really when you began to get the public anger [that] you realised that this was a great story and Coke had made a colossal mistake,' said Graham.

But even as they were fighting one media storm about the source of Dasani, another broke out just three weeks later. In the process of turning tap water into Dasani, calcium chloride was added for 'taste profile', and then ozone pumped through. The problem was that the batch of calcium chloride used had been contaminated with bromide, and the added ozone then oxidised it, transforming it into bromate, a nasty carcinogen. By the time Dasani was on the shelves, it contained 22 mg (0.0007/m) of bromate, twice the legal limit. Her Majesty's Drinking Water Inspectorate constantly monitor tap water for bromate levels and by coincidence had tested the Thames Water being supplied to the factory at around the same time Dasani was launched, finding it free of bromate. So Dasani, the health-giving pure water, was actually just Thames Water to which Coke had added a carcinogenic chemical.

Coke immediately called back the half a million bottles already dispatched to retailers, and this recall is thought to have postponed the introduction of the water to the rest of Europe.

All in, the blunder was reported to have cost Coke in the region of £40 million.

It was like watching a slow-motion PR car crash, recalls marketing expert Allyson Stuart-Allen:

'There was a 3,000 per cent mark up on Dasani. Now on the one hand you could say, "Wow, that's fantastic marketing." On the other hand, you have to defend that price position and to defend it you have to be more than just a purified water, you have to be something else.'

Coke argued that Dasani did have 'something else', but exactly what that was had been misunderstood. It wasn't simply tap water; it was the result of a 'highly sophisticated process' developed by NASA to create the purest drinking water you could get. In reality, though, the process, known as reverse osmosis, was already a common way of purifying water, and featured in consumer household water purification systems, having been developed without the aid of the US Space Agency. Things were starting to feel desperate.

How does a $45 billion company make such a hash of a drink of water? Says Allyson, 'With that sort of power comes a lot of hubris sometimes. Consumers are not foolish. They do know what's going on and they will find you out.'

I'M BACKING ~~PORTUGAL~~ BRITAIN

Grassroots campaigns are often heartfelt, but they have a habit of being strangled by weeds (and spotlight-craving politicians).

It's 1967. Britain is swinging. And so is the economy – at the end of a rope. With inflation rocketing and foreign exports tanking, Harold Wilson's government have had to devalue the pound by 14 per cent to be in with a hope of competing with European imports. It's humiliating for Wilson as he pleads no alternative to boosting output.

But five secretaries from plumbing manufacturers Colt Ventilation and Heating Ltd, in Surbiton, have a cunning plan…

On 27 December 'the girls of the typing pool' composed a collective letter to their boss offering to work an extra half-hour a day, for free, to do their bit for the economy and British-made products. 'We're Backing Britain,' they typed, in the process coining a pretty marvellous, media-friendly, rallying cry. The management didn't need persuading to take an offer of free labour (what management would?) and the week between Christmas and New Year being traditionally slow in terms of news, the story was a belated gift to the tabloids. So enthusiastic were the columnists and features writers who picked it up from the newsdesk that by mid-January 1968, 3,000 companies had announced that their workers were pledging to skip tea breaks to improve productivity.

Initially the movement was spontaneous and homespun so, naturally, politicians wondered what they might get out of it. Ted Heath, the Tory (and opposition) leader, hopped on the bandwagon followed by Prime Minister Wilson. Business leaders weren't far behind. Publisher Robert Maxwell launched a simultaneous Buy British campaign. He was passionate about all this, he said, failing to disclose that all the books he published were printed in Eastern Europe.

Meanwhile, the trade unions warned that the campaign was just a smokescreen for unpaid overtime. But that fell on deaf ears. And so, thankfully, did Bruce Forsyth's excruciatingly naff – but very catchy – single 'I'm Backing Britain'. It was rushed out to fanfare the movement and, in the spirit of things, everyone involved, including Bruce, made it for a reduced fee. It sold 7,300 copies and failed to chart.

Economically, experts said, the campaign was woefully naïve. It simply didn't add up. But for a brief moment it did have a bit of Dunkirk spirit, a feeling that the nation was pulling together and enjoying a collective experience not felt since, well, Dunkirk.

Badges, stickers and T-shirts were everywhere and festooned everything for the first months of 1968. London wholesaler Scott Lester ordered thousands of white T-shirts screen-printed with the 'I'm Backing Britain' slogan. But, it turned out, the shirts had been made in Portugal. Lester said, 'We can't find a British T-shirt which will give us the same quality at a price which will compare.' D'oh!

'I'm Backing Britain' disappeared almost as quickly as it arrived. The slogan remains in parlance only as the punchline of a joke, most famously Spike Milligan's quip: 'I'm Backing Britain – over a cliff!'

UP IN SMOKE

Cigarette advertising was banned on British TV in 1965, but cigarette manufacturers W.D. & H.O. Wills probably wished it had been much earlier. In 1959, a period in British history where you were in a minority if you didn't smoke, they launched a new brand, called Strand. The campaign centred on a costly TV advert that, to this day, still stands out for its artistry. It had a dishy protagonist, known in the script as The Lonely Man and in reality played by actor Terence Brook, a dead ringer for Sinatra. Wandering the empty streets of London at night, he stops to light a cigarette under a streetlamp. 'You're never alone with a

Strand' ran the tagline over a cool, downbeat theme jazz riff. It's not clear why he's mooching around in a trench coat in the early hours, but he looks good doing it. If you smoked Strand, the ad wanted you to know, you would reek of cool. The advert certainly struck a note with the public and brand recognition was extremely high. But something stank about Strand. Sales were a disaster. Most people who saw the ad translated its message into something akin to: 'Smoke Strand and you too can be a depressed, friendless loser.' The ad's soundtrack, called 'The Lonely Man Theme', was recorded by the Cliff Adams Orchestra and reached number 38 in the hit parade.

THIS DEAL SUCKS

When a company synonymous with vacuum cleaners decided to branch out as a travel agent, the result was an unmitigated disaster. Britons were swept up in Hoover's too-good-to-be-true special offer – and resorted both to hijacking and to Trojan horses to get their money back. Even the Queen was sufficiently miffed to whip back her Royal Seal of approval.

In 1992, the British division of Hoover had a surfeit of white goods, which they were desperate to shift. So they came up with the bright idea of offering two, free, round-trip airline tickets with every purchase of a Hoover product over £100. While the promotion was good only for trips inside Europe, canny customers realised they could make savings on flights.

Hoover didn't have their eye on the ball, though, and leapt from misguided to moronic by extending the offer to

US destinations. In 1992 a one-way ticket to the USA averaged £200, but Hoover were offering a pair of returns for £100. That made no business sense whatsoever. Their adverts acknowledged as much, running with a tagline that chuckled, 'Two return seats: Unbelievable.' Unusually for advertising, this boast turned out to be completely true – just not for the right reasons. More than 200,000 people bought Hoovers they didn't really want.

Hoover's European sales increased dramatically; their bottom line did not. Realising too late the calamity of the offer, Hoover refused to honour it. This incensed the public. In Cumbria, a Mr Dixon hijacked a Hoover branded van when a repairman from the company called to fix the dishwasher he had bought to fund a family holiday to the USA. Dixon refused to hand back the van until he got his tickets – and became a national hero overnight. BBC consumer rights show *Watchdog* became obsessed with the story and sent in undercover reporters to Hoover HQ. A grass-roots consumer group called the Hoover Holidays Pressure Group was formed and bought enough shares in Hoover's parent company to attend shareholder meetings and pressure them to pay up.

When that failed, the group took the company to the courts, making headlines throughout Europe and the United States. The court cases went on for five more years, costing Hoover £50 million and such a devastating drop in reputation that their owners, Maytag, were forced to sell off the company to an Italian competitor, Candy.

AT THE PICTURES: THE STORIES BEHIND THE SCENES

BISH! BASH! BOSCH!

Nestled in the Chiltern Hills, Turville is a tiny hamlet boasting the sort of chocolate box looks that have film location scouts swooning. To that end, its sixteenth-century stone cottages have been the backdrop to scores of TV dramas and feature films such as *I Capture the Castle* and *The Vicar of Dibley* (its church, Saint Barnabus, is actually Turville's St Mary the Virgin). The hamlet is cinematic shorthand for idyllic, pastoral England; a place where nothing changes, where time appears to have slowed. An inspired choice, then, for the location of the most shocking British film of the Second World War, a film intended as a rude wake-up for the nation.

Went the Day Well? was a British box office hit, released late in 1942. By the standards of the time, it was an extraordinarily graphic depiction of what might happen following a Nazi invasion of Britain. Some scenes – including a housewife attacking a man with an axe – still pack a punch today. Ealing Films, more famous for their comedies, produced the film and shot it on location at Turville, renamed as Bramley End.

The film tells the story of how a platoon of Nazi paratroopers is sent to soften things up ahead of a full-scale invasion of the UK. In June 1940, Germany really had drawn up plans to invade Britain, codenamed Operation Sea Lion. *Went the Day Well?* was deliberately intended to warn the UK populace that an invasion remained a possibility and that they must stay forever vigilant. It managed to deliver its warning positively and without scaremongering.

In the film, the invasion advance guard arrive mob-handed at Bramley End, disguised as British soldiers. Stationing themselves in the village, they're warmly greeted by the unwitting locals (mainly women and children). The soldiers are especially welcomed, and aided, by the local squire – a Nazi insider who knows their real identity. Soon, however, the women of the village begin to note that all is not as it seems about these Tommies. A *blink or you'll miss it* clue is the way that some of the squaddies write their numbers – in the Continental way, with a cross through the stem of a 7. Later, one of the soldiers publicly manhandles one of the kids. But what actually betrays the platoon is, of all things, a bar of chocolate.

'Schokolade? Funny sort of way to spell chocolate,' says a village boy on inspecting the legend stamped into the unwrapped bar. 'Yes,' chuckles his mother, 'that's the German spelling of…' The camera holds on her face as the penny slowly drops.

Die katze is now out of the bag, so the Nazis must now brutally suppress the villagers before anyone can escape and warn the *real* British army based some miles away. The women, children and pensioners of the village manage to mobilise and fight back, the action concluding at the manor house with a horrific shoot-out that could go either way.

Throughout the conflict, the Nazis remain in British khaki uniforms. Had the events depicted really have taken place, the soldiers would have been contravening both the Hague Regulations and the Geneva Conventions. Both state that it's legal for soldiers to be disguised in their enemy's uniform, but add that it's a war crime to go into combat without first removing that uniform and replacing it with their own.

Some in authority worried that the film would cause panic – especially as Brazilian director Alberto Cavalcanti drew on his background in documentary filmmaking to give parts of the film an almost fly-on-the-wall edge. Still, with average weekly cinema audiences of 19 million in 1939 – growing to more than 30 million by 1945 – that was a lot of civilians being alerted to the fact that any moment they might be called on to fight German soldiers, tooth and claw, outside Lyon's Corner House on the High Street.

As it turned out, the message of *Went the Day Well?* – to practice vigilance at all times – fell by the wayside. The threat of Operation Sea Lion had significantly waned by the time the film was released. Germany's 1941 invasion of the Soviet Union – starting with Operation Barbarossa – took precedence and was proving to be a costly mistake.

The film, though, remains a fascinating document of the times, and still has the power to shock. It was to prove the catalyst for many British films and books that dealt with the question of what would happen if the Nazis had invaded.

Bedknobs and Broomsticks did it with songs in 1971 (see page 64), but the1976 blockbuster *The Eagle Has Landed* is, to all intents and purposes, a remake of *Went the Day Well?* with a bigger budget and a couple of plot differences. Filmed at the beautiful village of Mapledurham in Oxfordshire, it's the story of German soldiers, led by Michael Caine, who are not an invasion force but simply ordinary squaddies (most definitely not Nazis) sent on a regular suicide mission to kidnap Churchill. They stick to the Geneva Conventions by removing their Polish uniforms when one of their number dies after saving a child caught in a waterwheel.

Len Deighton's alternative history novel *SS-GB* took the invasion to London and is a far less plucky – and more historically accurate – vision. The south of Britain is now under the jackboot, the rest of the nation will surely follow – and the round-ups have started. The stark choice is: collaborate, or die.

MCCARTHY'S CONTRIBUTION TO BRITISH CINEMA

In 1973 filmmaker Carl Foreman was nominated for an Oscar for his screenplay *Young Winston*, the story of one of the great figures of the twentieth century: Winston Churchill. Given a CBE for services to the film industry, it symbolised his status as British cinema aristocracy. Not bad for a homesick American who had been exiled from Hollywood 20 years earlier, and had his American passport revoked.

During the late 1940s and early 1950s, America was in the grip of an anti-communist witch-hunt lead by Senator

Joseph McCarthy. Suspected communists faced the House Un-American Activities Committee (HUAC), including leading names in Hollywood like Carl Foreman.

Foreman *had* been a member of the Communist Party in his youth but had left in 1941. Nonetheless the Committee ordered him to name other party members. He refused. That meant that he was blacklisted in Hollywood and his film career was over.

At the time he was working on *High Noon*, the powerful 1952 western about a town's principled lawman forced to face a bloodthirsty gang, alone. The film would receive seven Oscar nominations (winning four, including Best Actor for Gary Cooper) and is generally regarded among critics and audiences alike as one of the greatest films ever made. Many can identify with the dilemma at the centre of the film on some level, but Foreman, who wrote it, also lived it. Says film critic Matthew Sweet:

> *High Noon* is in a way a portrait of the turmoil in Carl Foreman's life at that moment. Gary Cooper is the marshal of a town under threat from the imminent arrival of a gang of killers. He's desperately trying to recruit deputies who'll help him defend the town. He goes to the church and he discovers that the population gathered there, who he has protected in the last few years, don't really want to help him. So this is a film about your friends not standing by you.

Some in Hollywood saw a message in *High Noon* they didn't like. John Wayne called it the most 'un-American thing' he had ever seen. Matthew explains, 'John Wayne looked at the last scene in the picture, where Gary Cooper throws down his marshal's badge into the dust, and he saw that as a symbolic rejection of American values. It was an act too far for him.'

Facing the moral quandary of naming names in front of HUAC, Foreman left the USA in 1952. He headed for London to try and set up as a scriptwriter – but with a very heavy heart, says his son Jonathan Foreman.

> He very much felt that he had been driven out. He knew, if he'd stayed, he wouldn't be able to work at all. There he had been, in America, the sort of Quentin Tarrantino of his time, hugely successful, especially after *High Noon*, and then suddenly it was all taken away.

Even in Britain, the blacklisting meant he had to write under pseudonyms. When he co-wrote another cinematic classic, *The Bridge On The River Kwai*, his name was left off the credits. Foreman's screenplay was based on the novel *Le Pont de la Rivière Kwaï*, which was written by French author Pierre Boulle. In spite of his amused admission that he couldn't even speak English, Boulle took the screenwriting credit so that Carl could avoid the blacklist.

Foreman's most ambitious film was the epic *The Guns of Navarone* about an Allied plot to blow up a German fortress. The film is packed with gung-ho action and adventure, and an outstanding turn by the English actor David Niven. But like *High Noon*, Foreman was writing on a number of levels, says Matthew Sweet:

> Essentially it's an antiwar picture. It has all the explosions, it has all those action sequences, but when the cast discovers

that the munitions they are going to use to blow up the super-guns have been sabotaged they question the whole point of the mission and the film turns into a kind of play about the rights and wrongs of war.

Winston Churchill didn't notice the subtle underlying message. He saw the film and loved it enough to request a meeting with Foreman. The main topic of conversation? How to turn Winston's early life into an action movie. It would certainly be an exciting film but Foreman had a concern, says his son John.

> He said to Churchill, 'You know I've had these political problems back in America, which is why I came here?' and Churchill sort of basically said, 'Oh my dear boy, don't worry about that, I don't care what a man believed when he was a boy, all I care about is if can he do the job.'

Churchill expected to see the finished film in a matter of months, as Carl Foreman related in a 1970s BBC documentary:

> So he said, 'You'll have it finished in two or three months, I suppose' and I said, 'No, sir, two or three years would be more like it.' 'Nonsense!' he said. 'When we decided on opening a second front in Normandy it didn't take us that long.' I said, 'Yes, you had more money.'

The film *Young Winston* didn't come out until 1972 – six years after Churchill's death – but Foreman was proud of it, calling it his love letter to England.

As the blacklist faded into insignificance, Foreman returned to work in America in 1975. Out with his kids he had a chance encounter with a former friend and fierce critic, remembers John. 'My father took my sister and I, walked us over to his table and John Wayne stood up, he was an enormous man, and they shook hands. It was weird… but it was a sign that things really were over.' Foreman was back where he felt he truly belonged. But, says Matthew Sweet, the British, especially the film business, benefitted hugely from his exile. 'I think that we should be proud that he worked here because if he had stayed in America he would have been condemned to silence.'

Carl Foreman died in Hollywood in 1984 aged 69 – a unique American who made some remarkably British films.

BRITAIN IN A SPIN

It had next to no budget, took six weeks to shoot on cheap 16 mm film and its controversial plot destined it to a graveyard slot on Channel 4. But when the TV play *My Beautiful Laundrette* was shown at the 1985 Edinburgh TV festival, the reaction to it was so rapturous that it was transferred to 35 mm and shown in cinemas. Now it was a proper film, and the next thing the cast and crew knew, it had received a nomination for an Oscar – Best Original Screenplay.

Set in the early 1980s and in a rundown corner of London, Omar (played by Gordon Warnecke) is a young British Pakistani in thrall to the Thatcherite dream of making money and being judged on your merits, not your background. He persuades his wheeler-dealer uncle (Sayeed Jaffrey) to hand over the keys to a rundown launderette. Omar sees a bright future in soap suds and plans to turn the mundane task of doing a wash and spin into a Las Vegas-like experience.

But as his launderette plans get spinning, his own dirty linen is about to be publicly aired. Omar's gay, from an ultra-conservative Muslim background and his wedding is being arranged. He's attacked by a racist gang, the leader of whom is his former lover, Johnny (Daniel Day-Lewis). It's a little awkward, but eventually the boys resume their relationship and realise the dream of the über-laundromat together, but racism, Omar's Muslim heritage and his impending arranged marriage all threaten to compromise their success. Will it all come out in the wash?

Written by Hanif Kureishi, *My Beautiful Laundrette* is a bittersweet and very funny observation of life in the entrepreneur economy of the 1980s. The story was partially autobiographical, Omar's dilemma being familiar to many first-generation British born Muslims who found it difficult – and dangerous – to balance their Western aspirations with what their immigrant parents expected of them. Gordon Warnecke, who played Omar, explains,

> I was fresh out of drama school and this was my first film. It tackled all the stereotypes of the time with real grit and humour, something I was really interested in doing, so this was a project I just had to be involved in. Thatcherite economics were key to *Laundrette*, and they were personal to me. We were part of the 'do it yourself' generation', surrounded by the spirit of free enterprise. But the film asks how far you can go before you find yourself torn between two cultures.

That Omar is gay – and largely unapologetically so, in private at least – caused consternation among the Asian Muslim community worldwide, for whom the issue of homosexuality is, by and large, taboo.

Director Stephen Frears was hooked immediately by what the film had to say about Britain in the 1980s.

> I read the script and just had to meet Hanif Kureishi. His mother was White British and his father was from Pakistan, so he lived and observed both cultures simultaneously. I mean, I was just white and middle class, so learning from him about that life was really eye-opening. I thought the critique of Mrs Thatcher was really the most important thing, I didn't notice that there were gay themes that were going to echo around the world.

But *My Beautiful Laundrette* doesn't preach, doesn't try to 'tick boxes' and has a magic 'common touch', which appealed to a wide audience. And Omar is constantly faced with the dilemma of whether he can eat the cake he has.

Souad Faress played Cherry, the manipulative Uncle Salim's wife, who questions where Omar's true identity lies. In the film she cries, 'I'm sick of hearing about these in-betweens, people should make up their mind about where they are!' Looking back, Souad says:

> I loved the script. Cherry's view is, 'Right, you have to side with us or side with them.' There's degrees of racism on both sides, but it made people at least look at the issues how they really are.

One thing that seemed to bewilder people was that the immigrant family, the Pakistani family, were so aspirational. They were a wealthy middle class family, but people just didn't equate immigrants with success, yet it has been proven over and over and over that in Britain's social history immigrants are very aspirational.

Powders – the name of the Launderette in the film – was on Wilcox Road in Vauxhall, south London. Today it's a Portuguese restaurant.

CUSHING THE BLOW – WHEN DR WHO BOMBED WITH THE FANS

In 1965, *Doctor Who* hit the big screen in eye-popping widescreen and retina-burning Technicolor, with Peter Cushing in the titular role. *Dr. Who and the Daleks* followed very closely the plot of 'The Daleks', the first, (black-and-white) encounter between the TV Doctor, played by William Hartnell, and the psychopathic pepperpots.

A sequel, *Daleks – Invasion Earth: 2150AD*, landed on screen less than a year later. Cushing again starred as Dr Who in the story that was, also again, a remake of a *Doctor Who* TV serial originally starring Hartnell. In both films, Cushing travels through time and space with three companions: his granddaughters, played by Roberta Tovey and Jill Curzon (the 1961 Women's Clay Pigeon shooting world champion, no less), and a companion who has stumbled on the Tardis by mistake. In the first film, this was Roy Castle; in the second, it was Bernard Cribbins, who would later play a significant role in the rebooted TV show during David Tennant's tenure.

The films were rushed out to cash in on the craze for all things Dalek that had swept the nation since their TV debut. Amicus, the producers, bought the rights to adapt the stories and characters from the BBC for £500. (The rights were limited, which explains why the famously spooky theme from the BBC Radiophonic Workshop – composed by Delia Derbyshire – is absent from the films and replaced by a racy, but rather ordinary, orchestral score). Terry Nation, the television writer who came up with the Daleks, had held on to the rights of his creation and was free to exploit his weaponised bollards with whomsoever he wanted. This is the reason the Daleks were also spun off into comic scripts that didn't feature Doctor Who characters.

In order to part-finance the second film, Amicus struck a £50,000 deal with Quaker Oats. In spite of being levelled by Dalek death rays, London is completely riddled with product placement: the huge billboard posters prominently displayed in the film suggest that in the far-flung future, the British eat nothing but, – surprise, surprise – Quaker's Sugar-Puffs.

The sets in both films are impressive, especially the post-Dalek-induced apocalypse scenes set in London. The Daleks – which, who knew cancelled, come in a variety of colours denoting rank – look twice as menacing in vivid colour. It's only a shame the proposed Dalek flame-throwers were nixed at the last minute in case they gave kids nightmares – or the wrong sort of inspiration for their homemade versions. Instead the Daleks in both films fire deadly gas (actually carbon dioxide from fire extinguishers).

The distinctive flying saucer in which the Daleks travelled to London – their evil plan to remove the Earth's core via a huge mine in, of course, the suburb of Shepperton – was dusted down and recycled three years later for the utterly terrible British sci-fi film *The Body Stealers*. That film starred Neil Connery – brother of Sean – and was probably responsible for his almost total screen obscurity since.

It has to be said, the Dalek films are far from classics – even the legend Peter Cushing delivers a ropey turn – but they do have a lot of charm and they don't even approach the awfulness of the TV *Doctor Who* of the mid to late 1980s. However both films drive 'true' Doctor Who fans to despair because – they say – Peter Cushing is an imposter. And it's true, the films took a lot of liberties with the *Doctor Who* legend.

If you weren't familiar with the TV show in the 60s – if you were American, say – you'd be flummoxed by the backstory, so the producers understandably simplified it for the widest possible audience. What was unforgivable for fans, however, is that Peter Cushing played a dotty *human* grandad who was an inventor not a Time Lord and whose surname was, actually, 'Who'. The true Doctor is extraterrestrial and nobody knows his name. The suffix 'Who' is applied by the people he encounters, as in 'Who are you?' That's the reason why you never see Peter Cushing included in the canonical lineup. You could argue that this all seems a bit churlish – after all, this *is* Peter Cushing we're talking about, one of the true greats of cult British films and also a cast member of the original *Star Wars* (and recently reanimated by CGI for *Rogue One*). However, there are some things in the universe you tinker with at your peril – and chief among them is the *Doctor Who* backstory!

ANY SIMILARITIES TO *MARY POPPINS* ARE PURELY COINCIDENTAL. HONEST!

An apprentice witch, a trio of cockney urchins and a cowardly spiv search for the missing component to a magic spell useful for thwarting the Nazi invasion of Britain. Not a recently released wartime MI5 file, unfortunately, but the plot of Disney's ballsy, brash comedy-musical *Bedknobs and Broomsticks*, tipped at the time to become an absolute classic of the studio's canon.

It had all the makings of one: a stellar cast that included Angela Lansbury, David Tomlinson, Roddy McDowall *and* Bruce Forsyth; a cracking set of songs by the Sherman Brothers; impressive special effects and animation sequences; classic baddies (in this case, the German Army); and orphans. It's a lovely, light-hearted fantasy worthy of Christmas classic status. So why did it fail to make back its productions costs?

Partly, perhaps, because it was so similar to *Mary Poppins* that the two merged in the consciousness of audiences. It featured the same star – David Tomlinson, Disney's go-to English twit; the same London setting; the same crew; similar themes (families are weird but they're all we've got); and stylistically *very* similar songs because they were written by the same songwriting team. Standout number 'Substitutiary Locomotion' is basically a rewrite of 'Supercalifragilisticexpialidocious', and 'Portobello Road' could have been in either film and few would notice the difference. In fact, another of its showstoppers – 'The Beautiful Briny' – had been written for *Mary Poppins* but was dropped at the last moment. In *Bedknobs* it was simply re-voiced for a frantic live action animated sequence that looked like a continuation of the one in... *Mary Poppins*.

The film was released in 1971, a week prior to the death of

Roy Disney, who had been in charge of the magic castle since his brother Walt died in 1966.

That's not to suggest that the film's lack of success played a part in his death – it opened strongly and was five times Oscar-nominated – but Roy's eye not being on the ball might explain why the film reached the theatres at an overindulgent (and hardly child-friendly) three hours long. A second release was cut to a more endurable two hours and then again to 90 minutes – with all but two of its songs excised.

Bedknobs was largely studio shot in California, including, sadly, the tremendous song and dance number 'Portobello Road'. There were, however, significant location scenes filmed at Corfe Castle and the surrounding village in Dorset. The three child stars were Roy Snart, now a software manager in Basingstoke; Ian Weighill, now a train driver; and Cindy O'Callaghan, last seen in *EastEnders* as Andrea Price and now a child therapist.

'My overriding memory is how well the three of us kids got on,' says Cindy, sitting down for a cup of tea with Ian and Roy for the first time in nearly fifty years. 'I don't remember any of us, however young we were, being naughty. It was a really professional engagement and Angela sort of set the tone. We upped our game because of her, she was very much an inspiration for me.' None of the kids could sing or dance when they were cast for an all-singing, all-dancing musical and Angela Lansbury's motherly encouragement could only go so far. 'Oh I was terrible, I was terrible then and an appalling singer now,' groans Roy, shaking his head. Ian concurs: 'I was a thirteen-year-old English boy, and I had to dance throughout the "Substitutiary Locomotion" song.'

During the animated sequence, the kids had no idea what was going on at all on what, to them, was a completely empty sound stage. 'All we could do was listen to the crew,' remembers Roy. 'They'd shout out, "There's a fish right next to you. Now talk to the fish!"' The overall experience, though, they all agree, was magic. In one instance literally. 'We did this one scene with the brass bed knob. We were all gathered around it and it turned pink, it was amazing.' Cindy was equally impressed, 'I remember! I still wonder how they did that, don't you?' Ray thinks he knows: 'It's easy, it's just Disney magic, isn't it?'

GOOD SPORTS

HEIL ZAT!

In Nazi Germany sport had one purpose, to strengthen the German people. But not all field games were acceptable to the Führer. Hitler thought the quintessentially British sport of cricket wasn't butch enough for his Aryan master race.

There is, apparently, a churlish but somehow characteristically Adolf reason for this.

It's reported that in 1923, having watched a team of British former prisoners of war play cricket and learnt from them the rules, Hitler raised a team to play against them. To his chagrin, Hitler lost. But what *really* incensed the would-be Führer was that he wasn't allowed to change the rules of the game. Whatever; Hitler's interest in cricket was short-lived. He may or may not have stormed off the pitch in a huff but he absolutely went on record to declare the sport 'unmanly'.

So, if he despised the game so much, why did he invite the Gentlemen of Worcestershire Cricket Club to Berlin for three games? And why might they have taken more than just wickets?

Some say cricket's complex rule book reflects the many

facets of genteel British manners – which a dictator might not want to adopt.

In 1937 Hitler – now the leader of Germany – dispatched his Minister of Sport, Hans von Tschammer und Osten, to London. During his stay the minister was invited to a lunch at Lord's, the home of cricket.

Von Tschammer und Osten reported this to Hitler, who came up with a cunning plan: challenge the British at their national game, and show the world that the Germans could beat them. The minister sent out an open invitation – worded, one suspects, more diplomatically than 'Would you like to be crushed and humiliated by the Master Race, weather permitting?' – and one club, the Gentleman of Worcestershire, accepted the offer to play in Berlin.

So it was that in August 1937 the Gentlemen found themselves in Berlin for the start of an unofficial Test-match series. As the team took to the field, they were asked to give a Nazi salute.

Good manners dictated that they did just that. But as the matches played out, the Worcestershire team were shocked by the lack of etiquette displayed by their Aryan opponents, who screamed 'Aus!' every other ball, probably in an effort to put Worcestershire off their stride. The English team also observed that the captain of the German side, Gerhard Thamer, would punch butter-fingered fielders who dropped catches off his bowling. We may all, at some point, have desired to do the same. But only a true barbarian actually would.

In spite of an intimidating backdrop of swastikas, anti-Semitic posters, the distant serenade of semi-automatic gunfire at night and being under the constant scrutiny of the Gestapo, the Gents went on to beat the Nazi cricket team in all three matches.

But in the midst of this extraordinary series, one team member may have had his eyes on more than just the ball.

Author Dan Waddell has researched the Nazi cricket series, and he discovered documents that suggest there was a British spy in their team. 'As I delved deeper into the story and started to gather information, there was one name that stood out. And that was this chap Robin Whetherly.' Dan says there wasn't an actual 'smoking gun' document identifying Whetherly as a spy,

> . . . but there's an accumulation of evidence that suggests it was likely. For one, he spoke German and he joined Special Ops during the Second World War and served with them, which again adds to this air of secrecy. He seemed to have no link to the Gentlemen of Worcestershire team, he never played cricket for them before. Finally, he flew out to Germany while the rest of them went on the train and he seemed quite separate to the rest. A few of the members didn't even know who he was.

Dan thinks Whetherly was embedded with the team to gather information and gauge the public mood in Germany at the time. 'The players spoke about watching a torch-lit procession, thousands of troops silently walking, apart from the beats of their jackboots on stone. That would have given him a real sense of the power of Hitler in Berlin at that time and of a nation gearing up for war.'

Nicholas Whetherly is the great-nephew of Robin and has some compelling, anecdotal evidence that suggests he made the cricket trip to Germany for more than the delicious promise of authentic strudel in the pavilion during tea. 'He went to Oxford, at the time notorious as a recruiting ground for spies and intelligence officers. That eventually led him to being appointed to Fitzroy Maclean's elite fighting unit during the war.' Nicholas is referring to the all-action super-spy Fitzroy Maclean, the man who may have been one of the inspirations for Ian Fleming's James Bond. During the Second World War, Robin served under Maclean on secret missions in Yugoslavia. 'Maclean's records credit and acknowledge my great-uncle as one of his original companions who had a first-class record as a fighting soldier.'

We'll never know for sure if Robin Whetherly was a cricketing spy. Within two years Britain was at war against Hitler, and in 1943 Whetherly was dropped behind enemy lines in occupied Yugoslavia on a secret mission. He was spotted from above by a Luftwaffe plane and killed.

THE REICH THING TO DO?

On 4 December 1935, Germany played England at Tottenham's White Hart Lane stadium. Before the kick-off the German squad gave the infamous Nazi salute as their national anthem played. In the stands 10,000 Germany away fans joined in. This seemed especially insensitive at the home of Spurs, a team with Jewish players and a huge following of British Jews. The rise of fascism across Europe and of the Black Shirts on the streets in the UK meant that there had been protests ahead of the game, and there are reports of minor disturbances inside the stadium as German fans were handed anti-Nazi leaflets. England won 3–0.

England's national squad played Germany again, this time in Berlin, on 4 May 1938. In spite of a growing public disquiet about British sides getting involved in politics, the team was ordered by the Football Association to 'heil' Hitler during the playing of Germany's national anthem. The players are reported to have been upset by the order and there was criticism in the British press – but in the crowd Hermann Goering, Rudolf Hess and Joseph Goebbels all looked on in pleasure. Until, that is, England beat Germany 6–3.

THE HAMPSTEAD WINTER OLYMPICS – SNOW JOKE

On 25 March 1950, a gloriously warm and sunny day, Norwegian skiers teamed up with the British Ski Association and built a ski jump on Hampstead Heath to hold a competition – with *real snow* packed and brought with them from Norway in massive chests.

Modern ski jumps reach 60–90 m (200–300 ft), but skiers on Hampstead Heath had enough room to jump to only about 27.4 m (90 ft). The jump itself was supported by a tower of scaffolding 18.3 m (60 ft) high, giving skiers a run-up of 30.5 m (100 ft) to the jumping point 3.7 m (12 ft) above the ground.

There was a live broadcast on radio and it was hoped this would be a regular event – a crowd of 10,000 turned up. The London Challenge Cup was open to all and was won by Arne Hoel of Oslo. This was followed by the Oxford vs Cambridge University Challenge Cup, which Oxford won.

The event made a comeback in 1951. This time there was to

be a grudge match with ski-jumping teams from the universities of Oxford and Cambridge.

In the 1950s very few people skied in Britain, let alone ski-jumped. But John Fox – interviewed for *The One Show* in 2015, when he was 85 years old – was one of the original three competitors jumping for Oxford. The memory of the 'Hampstead Alps' and the sheer crazy chutzpah of the event still makes him chuckle.

> They wanted to show the people of London what ski jump-ing was. It was exciting, of course, but I was anxious about the jump part because… we hadn't done that before! If you land on the flat, you come down with a bang and in those days there were no crash helmets, so we were taking a risk, I suppose. Thirty metres, I think, was my best – which wasn't bad, that's 90 ft. Surprisingly far when you think about it!

Wet weather for the second event in 1951 put off the crowds and put the kibosh on future events. Hopes that the Oxford and Cambridge ski jump competition would become an annual event – a kind of vertical boat race, if you will – literally melted away. In fact, there would be no British involvement in international skiing for a further four decades until Michael 'Eddie the Eagle' Edwards became Great Britain's Olympic ski jump competitor in 1988.

GREAT KOREA MOVES

1966 will forever be known as the year England lifted the World Cup trophy. Geoff Hurst's wonder strike in the last minute of extra time against West Germany may have got the headlines, but it was a different story on Teeside when a football team of North Koreans – known as the Red Mosquitos – caught both the imagination and the respect of the terraces.

1966 was the first time that North Korea had ever entered the World Cup and it was lucky that they got to compete at all. Official documents, released in 2010, revealed that the UK government, rather un-sportingly, moved to deny North Korea visas to attend. At the time the UK didn't recognise the state, which had proclaimed itself the Democratic People's Republic of Korea, (DPR) and feared that their attendance would cause political upset.

Fortunately the FA swerved a PR disaster by lobbying for them to play. The North Korean side were drawn to play their games in the North of England, and to be based in Teeside.

They arrived as complete football unknowns, but Middlesbrough fans took them to their hearts – possibly because, like their team, the Korea DPR (as FIFA knew them) wore a red strip. Dubbing them the Red Mosquitos, they cheered them on.

North Korea's first match saw them outclassed: the Soviet Union, their ideological comrades turned sporting enemies smashed them 3–0. Things picked up in the next match when they drew 1–1 with Chile. Amazingly, they triumphed 1–0 over Italy.

Back home in Italy, the shamefaced team were pelted with tomatoes and North Korean goal scorer Pak Do-Ik is, apparently, still referred to as 'The Dentist'. There are conflicting stories as to where this name came from, but one suggests that Pak was actually a dentist by trade.

That win meant Korea DPR would travel to Anfield in Liverpool to meet Portugal. Sadly, the Middlesbrough magic and goodwill didn't travel with them because they were beaten by Portugal 5–3. There is no truth in the oft-repeated rumour that the Korean team were sent to the coal mines when they returned home following that defeat.

WHEN THE REDS WERE UNITED

In 1915, a year into the First World War, it was decided to cancel all professional football fixtures for the duration. This was all very patriotic but, for professional players, who were paid per match and not at all between seasons, it spelt financial ruin.

In a backstreet Manchester boozer, an unlikely alliance was forged between a group of Manchester United and Liverpool players. The plan was to fix the result of the Good Friday match, on 2 April, between the two clubs. The players would all place bets on a 2–0 scoreline, not just locally but with bookmakers throughout the north and Midlands.

When they came to play, the match was so obviously thrown that supporters on both sides started booing within minutes of the start. It was difficult to distinguish who was really playing for whom. Penalties were deliberately missed and in one instance Liverpool striker Fred Pagman – who had refused to be part of the scam – was bemused when descended upon by angry teammates after he attempted to score against United. Luckily – for the conspirators since the score was already 2–0 – the ball hit the cross bar.

In spite of the consternation in the crowd, the match continued and later the conspirators cashed in. Bookies across the country were hit for huge sums of cash and started to cry foul after realising the unusually high number of 2–0 scoreline bets. (Scoreline bets were unusual at the time.) An investigation a month or so later by a suspicious book-making magnate exposed the scam. Matched to stories in the press calling professional footballers cowards for not joining the army, it led to all involved from being banned from playing football for life by the FA.

Contrary to what the papers alleged, however, many of the players had already decided to volunteer for action. Some were killed in service and others cited for their bravery.

In spite of this, it proved incredibly hard for those involved – some simply by association – to prove to the public that they had redeemed themselves, even though the Football Association reluctantly recognised that they would not have gone to such extremes if a salary system had been in place for professionals.

Manchester United's poster boy Sandy Turnbull, who had scored the first-ever goal at Old Trafford (a 4–3 loss against, ironically, Liverpool), was thought to be involved in the scam but was, in fact, entirely innocent. Lance Corporal Turnbull served with distinction with the Football Battalion and later the East Surrey Regiment, and was killed in the Battle of

Arras. Enoch 'Knocker' West, another Manchester United star, survived the war but spent the rest of his life protesting his innocence and appealing to the Football Association to retract their ban and the charges laid against him. His ban was finally lifted in 1945, when he was 59, but he has never been formally pardoned.

GREAT BRITISH HEISTS

GOING... GOING... GOYA

On the morning of 3 August 1961, at the kitchen table of 12 Yewcroft Avenue, Newcastle, 61-year-old Geordie retiree Kempton Bunton choked on his cornflakes. He had just read in the paper that the British government had paid £140,000 – approximately £21 million today – to keep Goya's Portrait of *The Duke of Wellington* in Britain rather than being sold overseas.

Kempton (named after the famous racetrack where his father had won a tidy sum six decades earlier) was enraged. This was a phenomenal amount of taxpayer's money to blow on a picture that could only be seen in London. How could it be justified? This former bus driver was now, like many pensioners, living on less than £8 a week, and from this he – and they – were having to fork out for the television licence.

Kempton was said to be an affable chap whose moral compass generally pointed north. But he was obsessed by the unfairness of the TV licence and campaigned to make television viewing free for pensioners. It was a lonely crusade, but you had to hand it to Mr Bunton, he had the courage of his convictions. He'd faced local magistrates twice over his refusal to pay for his TV licence – and his bloody-mindedness cost him a brace of short prison stretches.

On one occasion, he took direct action and snapped the 'BBC' button off his television set – much to the annoyance of his wife. In court for a third time, his argument had a certain logic. Since his act of vandalism meant he could now only watch the commercial ITV channel, why should he be expected to pay for the publicly funded BBC? His defence didn't cut any ice and he was sent down for another short stay. It looked like Kempton had run out of ways to stick it to the BBC. Until the morning he read about the Goya…

Kempton took a trip to the National Gallery, down in London, to see it for himself. It's there today and well worth a visit. This brilliant painting captures the Iron Duke – resplendent in uniform and covered in medals – in a surprisingly informal and intimate way. We don't know what Kempton's first impressions of it were, but he had plenty of time to form an opinion of it because the next day he stole it and took it back to his council house in Newcastle.

Given his age and weight (110 kg/17 st), how he did this is open to some debate. What follows is Kempton's version of events.

While at the National Gallery, Kempton struck up a conversation with a security guard, who spoke proudly of the costly, impenetrable, state-of-the-art alarm system that had just been fitted. The irony, the guard chuckled to the jolly, fat, bespectacled Geordie, was that at the start of each morning it was turned off for the cleaners. Later Kempton visited the gents' and wedged a small window open just a crack using a piece of cardboard. Early the next morning Kempton shimmied up the outside wall – conveniently there was a ladder in the alleyway below – and through the open toilet window. He then walked unchallenged to the painting, took it off the wall and returned to the gents'. All was going swimmingly until Kempton realised that the painting – in its fancy wood and plaster frame – would not fit through the window. He had to break the frame to fold the Duke and exit the window. Outside the gallery he separated frame from picture and threw the pieces of frame into the Thames. Later he retracted that and said he had hidden them in a cupboard in the London bed and breakfast where he'd been staying – he didn't want the landlady bothered by the police. (Kempton was considerate like that.)

Back in Newcastle Kempton wedged the painting behind the wardrobe in his bedroom. Goya's Portrait of *The Duke of Wellington* stayed chez Bunton for the next four years. Apparently, he never told his wife about the painting but did occasionally take it out for a private viewing.

With a national treasure as a hostage, Kempton immediately set about writing ransom notes – to newspapers, the police, the Home Office – laying out terms for its return. He was prepared to exchange it for, you've guessed it, a pot of money set aside to ensure the TV licence was free for people drawing a state pension. The recipients of Kempton's letters simply refused to take them seriously. This, after all, was an art theft that had clearly been organised by a criminal mastermind. Every organised crime gang between London and Palermo was disrupted by MI5 and Scotland Yard in the search for the missing masterpiece.

The case of the missing Goya gripped the nation. There was a £5,000 reward and it was a prominent in-joke for audiences of the first James Bond film, *Dr No*, when the painting, on display in Dr No's exotic lair, causes Bond to double-take.

All the time, it was stuffed behind a cupboard in a Newcastle Council house.

Colin Ashwell was a police constable in Newcastle in 1961. His beat took him past 12 Yewcroft Avenue daily. 'That's the thing that tickled me,' chuckles Colin, 'it was there the whole time. To be fair, these were tough, close-knit, working class neighbourhoods. There'd be plenty of domestics, but you didn't get many international art thefts.' Colin and Kempton had also exchanged pleasantries. 'He often had a grin on his face – now I know why! He was eccentric. I remember he was very passionate about the TV licensing issue. I think it drove his wife mad, though. I heard that when he snapped off the BBC switch on their TV she secretly got it out of the bin so she could watch what she wanted to when he was out!'

In 1965 Kempton took the Duke to Birmingham New Street station and placed him in a left luggage locker. He sent the ticket for this to the *Daily Mirror*'s newsdesk with a covering note that, for once, was taken seriously. And that's how the nation got the Duke back.

Kempton might well have got away with the whole caper scot-free. Incredibly, though, he presented himself to New Scotland Yard on 19 July 1965 and made a full confession. It turned out he'd told someone back home about his adventure, possibly after a few drinks, and was now worried he'd be shopped for the £5,000 reward money, even though the painting had since been returned.

The case went to the Old Bailey that November. 'After all that, he only got three months – and that was for breaking the picture frame, not stealing the painting. Kempton Bunton actually caused the law to be changed,' said former bobby Colin Ashwell, 'which got him a place in history, at least.'

Unwittingly, Kempton had benefitted from a loophole in the Larceny Act of 1916, which advised on theft cases. The Act stated that theft had to have evil intent – 'to deprive the owner thereof' for good. Kempton's ransom letters demonstrated that he had every intention of giving the painting back – so he couldn't, and wasn't, charged with its theft. It was a circumstance that had never occurred to anyone before – now it could easily be interpreted as a green light to Kempton copycats (or just plain opportunist thieves). With that in mind, the Theft Act (1968) was passed with a clause that made it illegal to 'remove without authority any object displayed or kept for display to the public in a building to which the public have access'.

After he served three months Kempton returned to Newcastle and spent the rest of his life without incident. He died, his remarkable story all but forgotten, in 1976.

The case may have been closed officially, but the question of how Kempton, over-weight and registered disabled, managed to remove the painting in the first place was never answered. Not, that is, until 2015 when a file in the National Archives was released. It details the arrest of a man from Leeds in 1969, who confessed to breaking into the National Gallery in 1961. His name? John Bunton. Kempton's athletic son had volunteered to 'borrow' the painting on his dad's behalf. John's lean physique made the job very easy, he said. When Kempton went to court,

John had begged him to let him take the rap, but Kempton refused on the grounds that it was his idea and he didn't want to get his boy into trouble.

THE TAKEAWAY REMBRANDT

The most stolen single painting in British history is in London's Dulwich Picture Gallery. It's Rembrandt's pocket-sized portrait, *Jacob De Gheyn III*. The portrait is a marriage of craft and beauty that measures barely 30 x 25 cm (12 x 10 in) – easily pocketable dimensions, which help explain why it's been stolen four times since 1966. On three occasions the painting – which has become known as 'the takeaway Rembrandt' – was simply swiped from the wall. It never stayed missing for long. It was found abandoned under a park bench, in a cemetery and in the back of a London cab that had been sent to Dulwich. Each time, it was returned anonymously. The last time that it was stolen, in 1983, the burglar put a little effort and flamboyance into proceedings and entered via the gallery's skylight. She/ he climbed down a rope, jemmied the painting from the wall and then escaped back up the rope and through the skylight. Although the painting at this point was too well known to sell on the underground art market, the Dutch work seemed to be gone for good. But three years later it was found lying on a luggage rack of a train at a British Army garrison in Germany.

MONEY TO BURN

Picture a bank heist involving hundreds of thousands of pounds, and it'll likely conjure up images of balaclava-clad men, complex blueprints and a getaway car. But tooling-up for one of Britain's biggest heists required nothing more than a roll of sticky tape and a pair of size 18 underpants.

It was a fiendishly simple and clever blag. The gang behind it could quite conceivably have kept coming back for more and gotten away with it. But criminal endeavours – even genius ones – do tend to rely on discretion, and that was in rather short supply.

Four married couples were involved, but we'll start somewhere near the end, with the main instigators – husband and wife team Peter and Christine Gibson.

On 17 January 1992, odd-job man Peter Gibson had arranged to meet the manager of a pension provider at his Essex office. His intention was to pay £100,000 into a pension for himself and his wife Christine.

Trouble was, he chose to make the deposit in cash, emptying out piles of crumpled and ripped bank notes from a plastic bag. The stunned manager grew even more suspicious when he then produced another huge wad of £50s from a leather holdall, waved it in his face like Loadsamoney (the Harry Enfield character, whose popularity was on the wane in 1992) and boasted that he was off to buy a car.

Following any large cash deposit, it is standard procedure for police to be informed, but there was nothing run-of-the-mill about the story that was about to unfold.

Peter Gibson liked his cars, as did his wife, Christine. But the 'salt of the earth' Essex couple also had a horse and enjoyed a jet-set lifestyle, with holidays from the Far East to Hawaii. 'A tad suspicious,' thought the police. And then they learned that Christine Gibson oversaw the burning of millions of pounds of reclaimed bank notes for the Bank Of England.

Destroying old notes is standard practice. There are only so many hands they can pass through before they become worn out. That might mean many years for a £50 note, but £10s and £20s have perhaps up to five years of use. Before £5 notes were withdrawn and replaced with shiny plastic sheets, you'd be lucky to get more than a year out of one. So they get sent back to where they started life, at the Bank of England.

Pam West is an expert on British bank notes and author of *English Paper Money*. 'They're all sent out in secure vans to a destruction plant in Essex, where nowadays they're all shredded into tiny pieces – but they used to be incinerated, with the resulting energy used to boost the central heating at the plant.'

Nobody was simply shovelling piles of cash into a fire pit. The plant was well supervised, there were checks and balances in place, and the routines were secure (relatively, it turns out). So the burning question was: how does anyone go about stealing money earmarked for the furnace?

The key was, well, a key.

The cash sat in cages – each cage secured by two padlocks coloured with either black or white tape. No one person possessed the keys to both black and white padlocks. Once the holder of the black key had removed their lock, Christine was cunningly able to swap it with a white one, to which she had the key, having disguised it with black tape. In that way, she could return and open both locks, gaining access to the money while she was on her own.

It was a crafty plan, but she still had to get the loot out of the bank.

Later, in court, it would emerge that she stuffed bundles of notes under her clothing and into her underwear, before substituting the correct padlock and casually clocking off with her bountiful brassiere. Exactly how she, and her co-conspirators, managed to avoid the Bank's random searches, however, will forever remain a mystery – most likely because banks try to keep their security procedures a closely guarded secret.

Within days of his ill-conceived trip to the pension advisor, Gibson, his wife and five other Bank of England employees were arrested. Anthony Boswood, QC for the prosecution, described Christine Gibson as the prime mover in the plan, and further commented that her husband Peter had not 'done an honest day's work in his life'.

One of those nicked, Kevin Winwright, immediately confessed to the theft of £170,000 and agreed to give evidence against his co-conspirators. The information he provided saw this unlikely gang end up at the High Court of Justice, where they stood accused of stealing hundreds of thousands of pounds from the Bank of England.

Christian Du Cann is the barrister who represented the Gibsons in the 1994 trial. 'It really was the most extraordinary case. It's estimated that between 1988 and 1992, the gang managed to steal at least £700,000 from under the nose of the Bank of England.'

You'd expect theft on this scale would come with some hefty prison time, but no. 'The Bank weren't able to take the case to a criminal court due to lack of evidence,' Christian recalls. 'Amazingly at that time, they had no way of knowing exactly or even approximately how much was stolen apart from through financial analysis. This was based on the huge discrepancies between the defendants' exorbitant spending and what they could prove they'd earned.' For example, the Gibsons could prove annual earnings of around £69,000, but in the same period the bank claimed they'd spent a whopping £300,000. It was a similar story with the others. The Bank of England had to pursue a civil, not criminal, case based on this and Winwright's confession.

Peter Gibson claimed that a lifetime of cash-in-hand work and dodging the tax man could explain their enormous income, but the judge presiding emphatically rejected these as 'wholly incredible and totally unsupported in any way'. He found the whole gang liable and ordered them to between them pay back just under a million pounds, including costs. Mrs Gibson and her husband Peter had to return £250,000; Kenneth Longman and his wife Janet, £150,000; and Michael Nairne and his wife Sharon, £110,000.

It ranks as one of Britain's most remarkable heists. While the one man who confessed to the crime was handed an 18-month sentence, the other members of the gang could walk free from court.

The Bank of England has now significantly tightened security and controls around the destruction of bank notes – but where there are big bucks at stake, you can bet that someone, somewhere will be trying to beat the system.

TOME RAIDER

William Jacques wasn't your average career criminal. He was quiet and understated, had studied economics at Cambridge and became a chartered accountant. But ultimately it was a different type of book-keeping he had his eye on.

His wanted poster should have read Public Libraries' Enemy Number 1.

While at university, Jacques got a taste for antique books and saw a novel get-rich-quick opportunity. The general public would never get access to these rare tomes but, by winning the trust of Britain's great libraries with his bookish air, Jacques gained access to handle their most valuable assets – and then nicked them. His method was hardly sophisticated. The scam was generally to stuff books under his jacket and walk out of the libraries.

Over a three-year period, Jacques stole an estimated £1.1 million worth of rare academic books, including first editions by Sir Isaac Newton and Galileo.

He'd sold his plunder through legitimate auction houses, but in 1999 it was a bid by a fledgling book dealer that stopped Jacques. Carl Williams was that student collector, now a highly respected dealer of rare and antiquarian books with an international client base.

Back then I saw this book by William Stanley Jevons called *The Logic of Quality*. Very rare, nice little book, and I bought it for, I think, £120. I took it to a book dealer some time later. And he said, "Can you leave it with me for a few days?" I was delighted, I thought, "Oh crikey, it must be good."

The dealer's experience and trained eye had told him something wasn't quite right, though. For starters, the book had been tampered with. If rare books have been in the possession of a library or specialist collection, they'll often have identifying marks on the spine, special labels inside the covers and embossed or blind stamping on the pages. Carl's copy of *The Logic of Quality* showed evidence that all three identifiers had been removed. 'So it was all there for him, it was obvious, forensically, that this book had been stolen. Obviously, that was very disappointing for me, but, at the same time, it was fascinating – a fantastic introduction to the book-dealing world for me.'

Having had his suspicions raised, the dealer turned detective. He learnt that only six copies of the book were in circulation and one of those was in the world-renowned London Library. He called them, asking them to check their shelves. Lo and behold, their copy was missing. He then called the auctioneers who had sold the book. They told him the seller was one of their regulars, William Jacques. One more call from the dealer to the London Library revealed that William Jacques was a member. Joining these dots together formed a picture that was very interesting to the police. When contacted by the police, Jacques fled to Cuba, leaving behind a letter listing safety deposit boxes around the country in which the police found 64 antique books, some worth well over £100,000 each. His motives for this were as mysterious as his sudden decision to leave Cuba and return to the UK, where he was arrested.

Jacques was not an easy criminal for police to read, but his book crime wave broke in front of the judge. During the trial Jacques revealed little about himself except that, disappointingly, his literary tastes were a tad more rip-roaring than his loot. He came to court every day clutching a Wilbur Smith adventure novel. And it wasn't even a first edition.

The evidence was overwhelming, and he had himself provided it by leading the police to the safety deposit boxes housing the rare – and reported stolen – books. Even so, Jacques denied he'd pinched them, claiming that he collected and repaired antique books as a hobby. However, he was found guilty and handed a four-year prison sentence.

Instead of turning over a new leaf on release, Jacques simply started a fresh chapter of pilfering. Because he was now the country's most recognisable tome raider, he returned to his old haunts incognito. Kind of; he'd grown a beard, wore his hair long and started wearing glasses. But the staff at the British Library clocked him almost immediately and he was asked to leave. So, he found a different place to steal his books, the Royal Horticultural Society's Lindley Library. Here he told them his name was Santoro and over the next three years helped himself to, among other horticultural classics, 13 volumes of the ultra-rare *Nouvelle Iconographies des Camellias* by the nineteenth-century Belgian author Ambroise Verschaffelt. Eventually he was spotted gingerly leaving the library with an angular bulge under his tweed jacket. The police were called. Searching him, they found an A4 'shopping list' of stolen books in his pocket.

On trial for the second time, the judge threw the book at him. Sending him down for another three-and-a-half years, he reminded Jacques that 'you are a Cambridge graduate and should know better.'

The Jacques cases are recognised as the catalyst that

tightened security in public libraries. Gone are the days of being able to stuff a tome up your jumper and awkwardly saunter out. But antique and first edition books are desirable and valuable assets that remain attractive to thieves willing to meet demand. In February 2017, £2 million worth of fifteenth- and sixteenth-century editions were stolen in a seamlessly professional heist by thieves who abseiled into a high-security warehouse in West London.

It's ironic that the people feeding the market for stolen books – the booksellers, librarians and collectors who know the commercial value of the material – are the very people who ought to know the cultural value of the books, and the importance of making them available to the public.

Policing the trade in stolen books are agencies such as the Antiquarian Booksellers Association, and they're making things much harder for the itchy-fingered minority in the book-theft game. ABA's online stolen books database is enormous and full of forensic detail about hundreds of thousands of individual editions. They help global libraries and collectors alert the legitimate book trade to heisted books the moment they go missing. 'Books are surprisingly individual, even pages from books are remarkably easy to identify if somebody's done their cataloguing properly in the first place,' says ABA's Tim Bryars. 'So if you're trying to deal with stolen material, the police are now very ready to act.'

CRIME DOESN'T PAY

A selection of some of the books pilfered by Jacques, and their estimated value today:

Newton *Philosophiae Naturalis Principia
Mathematica* (1687; two copies) **£100,000 each**

J. Kepler *Astronomia nova* (1609) **£65,000**

J. Kepler *Tabulae Rudolphinae* (1627) **£14,000**

G. Galileo *Sidereus Nuncius* (1610) **£180,000**

G. Galileo *Dialogo* (1632) **£28,000**

T. Malthus *An Essay on the Principle of
Population* (1798) **£40,000**

N. Copernicus *Astronomia instaurata* (1617) **£7,500**

C. Huygens *Traité de la Lumière* (1690) **£15,000**

Smith *An Inquiry into the Nature and Causes of the
Wealth of Nations* (1776) **£2,000**

J. Napier *Mirifici Logarithmorum Canonis
Descriptio* (1614) **£16,0000**

ONE OF OUR GORILLAS IS MISSING

During the 1930s and 1940s, Alfred the Gorilla was Bristol Zoo's poster boy. Arriving from Africa as a baby, Alfred had plenty of character and helped reverse the zoo's fortunes, boosting their visitor numbers. He was widely mourned on his death and all 2.1 m (7 ft) and 272 kg (600 lb) of Alfred was stuffed and given pride of place in Bristol's city museum. To this day, visitors make a beeline to Alfred's final resting place. In 1956 three students carried out a precision-mapped raid on the city museum to steal Alfred. Their plan included hiding out overnight in a bell tower and was so well executed that, had they turned their efforts to a bank vault or picture in a gallery, they would surely have been the toast of HM Prison Pentonville. In fact, the trio smuggled the misappropriated ape back to their flat, and took a series of photos of him in amusing poses – some featuring themselves, which would have been hard to explain. Two days of monkeying-about later, the lads transported Alfred to a nearby doctor's surgery, where they left him in the waiting room. Since then Bristol was gripped by conspiracy theories as to the truth behind Alfred's Lost Weekend, but the true story came to light in 2010, when Ron Morgan, one of the original kidnappers, died. Partner-in-crime Fred Hooper confessed to the press and released the photos of their captive. The identity of the third kidnapper, known only as D.S., remains a secret to this day.

GONE TO THE DOGS

Petrol rationing in Britain during the Second World War and in the years after meant that horse racing was severely restricted by the cost of transporting horses across the country. Dog racing took the lead in terms of the nation's favourite flutter. With more than 70 dog tracks operating at that time, there was a lot of cash floating around – always an interesting proposition to the less than honest.

David Stuart Davies is a novelist and historian who lives and breathes the criminal underworld of the 1940s and 1950s.

There's an idealised view of a 'we're all in this together' mentality during the war years, but in fact crime figures rocketed. And with annual attendances for dog-racing in the '40s in London alone touching eight million, the dog track provided the perfect arena for all sorts of nefarious activities. Despite the tracks employing their own private police force, many of whom were ex-Scotland Yard, the sheer scale of the crowds afforded anyone with criminal leanings the possibility to merge into the crowd and avoid being spotted.

The consequences were inevitable: 'The tracks became a natural trading ground for black-market deals: stolen or forged documents, like petrol coupons, identity cards and ration books would be available.' But it was betting and the money associated with it where most criminals focussed their interests. 'It was a very rich seam for scammers who could forge betting tickets or dope dogs to bring in large wins.'

On 8 December 1945, at White City dog track in London, a previously unlisted dog, Bald Truth, was added at the last minute to make up the numbers in the last race of the evening.

What happened next would amaze the dog's owner (who appeared to be completely unwitting of what would unfold), enrage 16,000 race-goers and cost bookies across Britain an estimated £100,000 – £2.5 million in today's money.

Five dogs, all in good health, were raring to launch from the starting traps. But, just before the automated hare began its speedy circumference ahead of the pack, a wave of anxiety swept through the rows of bookmakers. The rank outsider, Bald Truth, quoted at 20:1, had suddenly dropped in price to 5½:1. People were throwing money on at the very last instant. They also placed bets at other dog tracks right across the country, from Manchester to Birmingham and even as far away as Newcastle. It was a classic scam, 'little and wide'. Most bookies were stunned but had little choice to take it on the chin.

What happened next?

'The traps flipped open... the dogs, bunched close, skidded the first bend... then the four brown bodies slowed to a bewildered, pathetic gallop... obviously doped. Bald Truth swept past the winning post 15 lengths ahead.'

So wrote Superintendent Robert Fabian in his memoirs (see page 28 for more Fabian adventures). Fabian was a copper of the old school, well respected on either side of the law and the inspiration for the BBC's first police procedural crime drama, *Fabian of the Yard*. He'd been called in to investigate how the mickey had been slipped to the dogs.

In a very narrow gap in the seemingly boarded-up kennels, Fabian found clothing fibres torn from an expensive suit. The interloper would have had to hide himself inside overnight and sneak out at an opportune moment to drug the dogs, before hiding back in the kennel and sneaking out again only once the stadium was shut for the evening. He would either have been a child – unlikely given the cut of his cloth – or a very slender man. Fabian said in his memoirs that he knew who it was immediately: his nemesis and 'the coolest crook in London' (as well as the skinniest), London Johnny.

The evidence started to stack against London Johnny, a notorious doper of dogs, when he was witnessed flashing the cash with his equally roguish mate, Eddie Chapman. Eddie was heard to boast about taking White City, which probably confirmed the theory for Fabian. But something weird happened. No arrests were made, no case was brought, no money recovered. Eddie Chapman was, however, banned from every dog track in the country – without explanation.

To 'the powers that be', Chapman was better known by the

codename Zigzag and was one of Britain's greatest, certainly bravest, double agents. In the 1930s Chapman had been a safe-cracker – the first in Britain to use gelignite – and high on Scotland Yard's Most Wanted list. He was arrested in the Channel Islands – on the eve of the Nazi invasion. Overnight he became a prisoner of the Nazis.

Chapman then convinced them that he hated the British, who only ever wanted to lock him up, and insisted that he could be a useful asset. After some feats of espionage, he became the only British national to be awarded the Iron Cross. In fact, however, he had become a double agent for the British at the earliest opportunity, and much of what he reported and claimed to have achieved was elaborately faked by MI6.

What's this got to do with dog doping? Well, there's no proof, but it's probable that Eddie, bored after seven months of peace, turned his guile and cunning to the racetrack and teamed up with London Johnny for some fun. They were caught and by rights should have been tried. But in court could he be trusted not to mention the still highly Top Secret operations in which he had been involved? That aside, the nation genuinely owed Chapman – his work saved thousands of lives. The likelihood is that quiet words were had from the top down. Eddie's ban from Britain's dog tracks was probably a compromise. Either way, he seemed to have retired from crime soon after and opened a luxury health spa with his wife.

What we do have some certainty about is how London Johnny and Eddie Chapman (allegedly) managed to turn a pack of well-trained greyhounds into jelly that night. Fabian's investigation found pieces of fish that had been laced with a substance called Chloretone. In humans, this can used to suppress motion sickness. Give it to a dog and the effect is very different. Its blood pressure will rocket but only when its heart rate increases rapidly – at, say, the moment it has left the trap and hit the first corner. Once that happens the reaction is an almost immediate collapse. It was the perfect dope: undetectable during a medical, quickly effective and non-fatal.

GOLD RUSH

Want to know what happened to the Brink's-Mat gold? You're wearing it.

On 26 November 1983, a gang broke into the Brink's-Mat warehouse at Heathrow airport. Their target was £3 million in cash and they'd been helped by an inside man. What they actually found was diamonds and £26 million in gold bullion – pure, 24-carat gold. Christmas had come early.

Once they'd got the loot to a safe place, they considered their haul. It was essentially worthless.

The trouble with sizeable quantities of pure gold is that they are very difficult to shift without raising eyebrows. Especially in the quantity we're talking about. On a practical basis alone, it's heavy stuff; a single, standard bar of bullion weighs 12.4 kg (more than 27 lb). If Michael Caine and his gang in *The Italian Job* had been throwing around real bricks of bullion, they'd have been in hernia hell before they could get the motors of their Mini Coopers running.

In the real world, no legitimate gold dealer or goldsmith will touch pure gold without the requisite paperwork – and even then there are problems because pure gold is simply too soft for making jewellery. (Dental gold, which has been used for hundreds of years to fill cavities, is almost pure, however. So if you have gold fillings – and if you're of a certain age – you might well refuse your dentist's kind offer of disposing of them for you.) Twenty-four carat bullion is 1000 parts of gold per 1000 parts of gold, and therefore the most expensive – that's why most bullion rarely sees the light of day. It generally just moves from bank vault to bank vault as a commodity for trading. All the gold that's ever been produced, would fill a hole only the size of a tennis court and 9.75 m (32 ft) deep. Gold used for jewellery is endlessly recycled

The gold that jewellers buy to work with is generally between 18 and 12 carat, and has been cut with other metals such as silver to make it harder. Diluting gold brings the carat down and makes it go further, too. The lowest carat – cut with less precious metals – is nine, which equals 375 parts of gold per 1000 parts. In most Asian countries nine carat is considered so dilute as to not even be gold, but it's perfectly acceptable as such in Europe.

The Brink's-Mat gang had to find ways of shifting their loot undetected. One simple – but highly risky – method was to advertise the gold as legitimate in trade papers and pawn shops and offer it at extraordinarily low prices. They also recruited goldsmiths on the shadier fringes of the trinket trade to turn the bars into jewellery. All this was taking a long time, so they decided that lowering the carat of the gold would make it untraceable, enabling them to sell it on quickly.

To bring down the carat of gold takes knowledge and skill. You also need access to a smelter. Kenneth Noye, an Essex 'businessman', was now involved with the gang and ticked those boxes. He had some knowledge of how gold 'works', and he knew a man with a smelter – John Palmer, who was later cleared of knowingly handling the stolen bars. To reduce the carat the gang began to shovel bag loads of two pence pieces (which are made of copper), old jewellery and silver candlesticks into the smelter where, at 1064°C (1948°F), the bullion turned liquid. This method was clearly successful in some part – three tonnes of it is still missing, after all – but bars were recovered with unmelted coins clearly visible.

The gang were anything but subtle. Some members immediately went out and bought ostentatious cars and houses, and one even bought a pair of Rottweiler puppies and called them Brinks and Mat. And when Noye walked into a High Street branch of a bank in Bristol and withdrew £3 million – a sum so large that the Treasury had to be informed – the police put Noye under surveillance, leading to the case being finally cracked.

To this day, significant quantities of the gold are still missing, the only aspect of the case that remains open. The hunt continues, but some people say the answer is under our noses, or on our fingers. The gold that got away was laundered back into respectability – so well, in fact, that every piece of gold jewellery produced in this country since 1983 has an element of Brink's-Mat bullion.

BLOOD'S GUTS

For more than 300 years, they were undisturbed by light fingers. So confident of their security was the newly installed Charles II that the Crown Jewels became a hot seventeenth-century visitor attraction.

One ticket-buying tourist was the Irish soldier Captain Thomas Blood, who gained his rank in Cromwell's army, having swapped sides when things were going badly for the Royalists.

Blood was a rogue with a reputation for applying his military nous to well-planned scams. But his attempt to pilfer the Crown Jewels – newly commissioned by Charles II after Cromwell smelted the originals – took things to a different level.

Over a matter of weeks Blood, pretending he was a pastor, visited the Tower daily, becoming friendly enough with the Master of the Jewel House, Talbot Edwards. Eventually he was invited to dine. Building on this trust, Blood introduced Edwards to members of his 'family', who also became dinner guests. After one pleasant evening of imbibing, Blood persuaded the guard to treat them all to a private viewing. Once they were all alone in the treasure room, Blood and his men overpowered the Master, tied him up and set about relieving the Tower of its booty. In the process, many of the treasures had to be bent and flattened in order to fit in the swag bags.

Blood would have got away with it if Edwards' son hadn't suddenly arrived on the scene. History records that he was tasty in a fight and managed to subdue the entire gang. Once arrested and imprisoned – in the Tower – Blood refused to speak to anyone but the King. Charles II clearly admired Blood's guts; he granted a private audience and then not only pardoned Blood but threw in a pension, too. Blood apparently informed the King that the jewels were worth only £6,000 (at seventeenth-century prices) not the

£100,000 declared by the Crown. A conspiracy theorist or even a loss adjuster might briefly ponder an insurance scam as a line of enquiry – but don't let cynicism get in the way of good roguish yarn.

GREAT ESCAPES

EARL'S CAUGHT IN THE ACT – THE HUNT FOR MARTIN LUTHER KING'S ASSASSIN

Dateline: April 4 1968, 6.01p.m., Memphis. The American Civil Rights leader Dr. Martin Luther King Jr is assassinated.

In a nation riven by racial tension, where some states enforced a system of apartheid little changed since the days of slavery, Dr King's mission was to establish equality for African-Americans through non-violent protest and dialogue. On 4 April he was in Memphis to lend his support to striking African-American sanitation workers in the city. Dr King was killed as he stood on the balcony of the Lorraine Motel just feet from his room, number 306. He was hit by a .30-06 bullet fired from a Remington 760 rifle positioned across the street.

The murder sent shockwaves across the world and was met with despair at home. Just five years earlier King had famously announced his dream – a dream of equality, outlined to an audience of more than 250,000 people gathered in Washington DC. Now, as rioting erupted across the nation, American had woken to a nightmare.

The FBI were mobilised for what would be the largest man-hunt in their history. There *was* an early breakthrough. A Remington 760 rifle was found abandoned near the scene. It bore the fingerprints of a career criminal and known white supremacist – James Earl Ray, who also happened to be on the run from Missouri State Penitentiary.

But Ray had already made it to Canada and was busy changing his identity.

Using a fraud seemingly ripped from a pulp-fiction paper-back, but already well established among US citizens attempting to dodge the draft for the Vietnam War, Ray found the name of a Canadian citizen called Ramon Sneyd in the Toronto phone book.

Borrowing the name and address of Mr Sneyd, Ray was able to apply for a replacement birth certificate. With that, a Canadian passport was plain sailing and Ray was able to fly to Lisbon – via a stop-off in London – where he was hoping to join a band of white mercenaries fighting in what was then Rhodesia (now Zimbabwe), and which had no extradition treaty with the USA at the time.

Although Ray would have passed through at least three passport and security control checks, no officials noticed that there was a typo on the false passport, which had been issued in the name of Ramon Sneya, not Sneyd. Ray's hand luggage wasn't searched, either; otherwise his smuggled .38 revolver would have been discovered.

In Lisbon, Ray's proposed meeting with the mercenaries fell through. He stayed a few days but didn't speak Portuguese, so he returned to London to work out what to do next. Before he left, however, he visited the Canadian consulate, which helpfully issued him with a new, correctly spelt passport for Mr Sneyd. Ray kept both passports. A poor decision, it would transpire.

Meanwhile in the USA, the FBI had worked out Ray's passport ruse – but until they'd cross-referenced thousands of photographs they had no idea what name he'd taken or where he was. Still, they had enough information to issue Wanted Posters across the world.

Back in London, Ray was hiding in a succession of dives in Earl's Court. During the 1960s it was a perfect place to hide in plain sight. Earl's Court was central but rough and ready, full of cheap hostels and B & Bs. It was a magnet for thousands of young Australian travellers – hence its nickname Kangaroo Valley – so Ray's southern US drawl made him memorable to those he met.

With just a cheap paperback spy-thriller (Cameron Rougvie's *Tangier Assignment*) and his pistol wrapped in a spare T-shirt in his suitcase, Ray kept a low profile, venturing out to wander the streets and make the occasional telephone call to try and make contact with the Rhodesian mercenaries. Three weeks into his English vacation, though, James Earl Ray was short of money and growing paranoid that the net was closing in on him. He was ready to take a drastic measure, one that would thrust an unlikely couple into the story.

Maurice Isaacs and his wife Billie were the middle-aged proprietors of trinket shop Treasures of Paddington, located on Praed Street, Paddington. An otherwise normal day in the trinket trade was rudely interrupted by a gun-wielding visit from the world's most wanted man. But rather than give in to Ray's demands for the shop's jewellery, Maurice grabbed

Ray's arm, pushing the pistol towards the ceiling, and Billie steamed in, delivering a painful boot between the legs. Ray turned tail and ran.

His mini crime spree continued, though. He went on to rob the TSB bank on Earls Court Road – getting away with £90, just enough to get an air ticket to Brussels. The final hurdle was Heathrow's passport desk, which Ray was confident he could breeze through as he had done on three occasions since leaving USA. But at the desk he fumbled, pulling both of his fake passports out at the same time. Both identical bar one single letter.

'Are you,' asked the customs man, 'Mr Sneya or Mr Sneyd?'

Ray laughed and said it was 'just a typo', which cut no ice because Ray was asked to follow the officer to an interview room where he was searched. His gun was found. Ray couldn't provide a licence, let alone an excuse.

Scotland Yard were called and dispatched one of their most famous detectives – Chief Superintendent Tommy 'One Day' Butler. The 'One Day' soubriquet came from his reputation of cracking a case in 24 hours.

Butler, who had led the Flying Squad team that cracked the Great Train Robbery case, presented Sneyd with a copper's hunch. A hunch, to be fair, that benefitted from an international, all-points bulletin issued by the FBI earlier that week and featuring photographs, descriptions and a statement that James Earl Ray was travelling under the name Sneyd and was likely to be in London. Martin Luther King's murderer cracked and confessed. 'I feel so trapped,' he cried, as Butler arrested him.

To speed up extradition back to the States, Maurice Isaacs and the TSB quietly agreed to drop the charges of armed robbery against James Earl Ray. After being held and processed in the UK, detectives from Memphis flew to Heathrow to collect him. He was flown back in chains.

James Earl Ray was eventually sentenced to 99 years in prison. He died, still incarcerated, in 1998. He'd tried to silence King's message with a gunshot. He failed. The reverend's sermon of hope is still as loud, and vital, today.

THE MAN THEY COULDN'T LOCK UP

Nearly 300 years ago, 200,000 people lined the streets of London to witness the final journey of Britain's most popular crook.

He was so famous that Daniel Defoe, author of *Robinson Crusoe* and chronicler of the age, detailed his every exploit in a bestselling biography.

Our hero's name was Jack Sheppard. He was the rogue's rogue; if it wasn't nailed down, Jack Sheppard would pinch it and you, taken by his cheeky aplomb, would thank him for it. But he was most famous for his talent for escapology, a faculty that propelled him from mere petty thief to living legend. It's quite possible that a third of the population of London came out for Jack's execution not to see him dangle from the end of a rope but to escape it.

Jack was handsome, baby-faced with quick charm and wit. He gave criminality not exactly a good name but certainly an attractive one, and was a trusted and popular figure among the underworld villains of eighteenth-century London.

Young Jack was apprenticed to be a carpenter, but found drinking, gambling and stealing offered better prospects. With his brother, Tom, he embarked on a series of burglaries in central London. After robbing a linen shop, Tom was caught and to avoid punishment turned grass on his brother. Jack was arrested and imprisoned in the Roundhouse in St Giles, a prison in the centre of the then notoriously lawless London borough known as the Rookery (near where Centre Point now stands). His incarceration didn't last long. Within hours he'd broken through the ceiling of his cell, run along the prison roof and jumped down into the crowd that had gathered below to investigate the source of tiles and masonry falling from the prison.

The law caught up with Jack when he and his mistress, Bess, attempted to steal a pocket watch. The pair ended up sharing a prison cell and didn't waste any time in getting between the sheets so that they could tie them together to make a knotted rope. That seems like a movie cliché now but, says record-breaking escapologist Stuart Burrell, it was the first recorded instance of such an escape method.

> He was a true innovator, years ahead of his time. But it wasn't an act. The modern feats that you attribute to Houdini were 180–200 years away. Stories of Jack were really entering into the public's consciousness. But people were at a loss to explain how he was actually performing the escapes, the feats he was becoming famous for. In fact, one story even has the Devil himself acting as his assistant.

Jack's secret, says Stuart, was that he had amazing physical strength but also that he'd obviously been paying attention during his carpentry apprenticeship. 'It gave him a detailed knowledge, not only of woodwork and locks but also metal-lurgy. If you gave him even the most rudimentary tool he would find a way to use it to engineer his escape.'

Jack relished running rings around his captors, but it was when the rogue carpenter came to the attention of Daniel Defoe – the most famous hack of his age – that he entered into nationwide legend. Jack's third prison break, reported a delighted Defoe, caught the authorities with their pants down. Held in the condemned cell of the heavily fortified Newgate prison, he had only a regiment of prison guards for company, but Bess smuggled in a set of ladies' garments. Jack dragged up and simply sauntered out, unquestioned, to freedom.

Historian Lucy Moore says that his next escape was truly spectacular. Rearrested and thrown back into the condemned cell at Newgate, Jack investigated the fireplace and managed to extract an iron bar, break through the chimney, climb up the flue to the floor above and then break through six other locked rooms to the outside wall of the prison. On the point of escape, Jack realised he couldn't get down the sheer outside wall. 'So he made his way all the way back to where he started, collected his bedsheets and returned to drop down the outside wall.'

Reports of this made Jack a folk hero, but the authorities had had enough. He was caught after being found in a tavern very smartly dressed but dead drunk (the profits of turning over a pawn shop in Drury Lane two days before). Jack was sentenced to death at Westminster Hall and sent to Newgate – again. This time he was placed in a cell where he could be observed at all times from all angles. Just to make sure, he was weighed down with 136 kg (300 lb) of iron chains. As he awaited his fate he became a visitor attraction at the gaol and a source of revenue for the guard, who charged the gentry four shillings a peek. James Thornhill, King George I's personal artist, even painted his portrait in the cell.

Jack's execution was planned for 16 November 1724. He was, of course, plotting one last escape. The plan was that a group of friends would rush the gallows and cut him down as the platform under his feet gave way. Jack's fame proved to be his downfall, however. His friends couldn't get through the teeming crowds in time to save him.

THE MAN THEY HANGED JUST KEEPS ON SWINGING

In death, the Jack Shepppard legend only grew. The poor found inspiration in him, and the establishment feared his influence – to the point that plays about him, or even characters in plays named after him, were banned by the Lord Chancellor until the 1740s. This may explain why the central character in John Gay's *The Beggar's Opera* (1728) is clearly based on Jack Sheppard but is called Macheath. Bertolt Brecht and Kurt Weill's *The Beggar's Opera* in 1928 featured their own homage to Macheath/Shepherd – 'Mack The Knife'. Now a jazz standard in its own right, 'Mack the Knife' was a hit for Louis Armstrong in 1956, established Bobby Darrin on the world stage with his 1959 cover and won Ella Fitzgerald a Grammy in 1960 with a version she improvised after forgetting the lyrics during a live recording in Berlin. Simon Cowell has gone on record to say that 'Mack The Knife' was the 'best song ever written'.

HAIN IN THE FRAME – TRUANT HELPS LORD AVOID JAIL

In the early afternoon of 24 October 1975, a man walked into a branch of Barclay's Bank in Putney, southwest London and stole £490 from an open till.

There were plenty of eyewitnesses in the bank, and the robber was then seen getting into a car with a clear number plate. He was traced, arrested and later picked out in an identity parade.

The suspect in this seemingly open-and-shut case turned out to be a well-known student radical. He was Peter Hain – now Baron Hain of Neath, former Secretary of State for Wales and one of the brokers in the Northern Ireland Peace Process.

Back in 1975 Peter Hain was a student radical, dubbed Hain the Pain by the tabloids, such was the frequency of his noisy appearances. An ardent supporter of the anti-apartheid movement, he actively protested against the South African regime and institutions that did business with them – like Barclays Bank.

So was the Putney job the ultimate student protest? In short, no. Hain had demonstrated outside that very bank in the past, he'd even been photographed by the press doing so. It would have been pretty stupid to rob it. Yet he came perilously close to being convicted for just that.

He lived close to the bank. In fact, the morning of the robbery he was in WHSmith on the same street, buying a typewriter ribbon. He was tucking into his lunch at home when the police arrived and arrested him for robbery. The severity of the charge didn't immediately register. Peter asked if he could finish his sandwich, and was given short shrift.

Hain was detained in the cells, even though the police didn't seem to have that much to go on.

A fingerprint was recovered from some of the stolen money known to be handled by the robber – but it wasn't Hain's. The witness statements were also confused. Meant to be describing the same man, they reported that he was 'wearing an everyday white shirt', 'a blue shirt with puffed sleeves', 'a checked shirt'; he 'was wearing glasses', 'wasn't wearing glasses'; 'Aged 23', 'about 33'; 'His complexion was Egyptian', 'was definitely European'; 'Spoke with a Spanish accent'; and 'had black curly hair that flowed to his shoulders', 'just below his ears', 'definitely short, brown hair', 'a bit gingerish'.

Nonetheless the police ordered an identity parade for the next morning. Overnight someone in the police station let the press know that Peter Hain had been arrested for bank robbery. London's *Evening Standard* front page that morning featured a large photograph of Hain, the story of the robbery and news that he was to take part in an identity parade. All of the witnesses asked by the police to take part in the parade said later that they had read the *Standard*'s coverage before arriving at the police station – where there were even copies in the waiting room. Today that leak to the press would have rendered the lineup unsafe and the case would have been thrown out. But in 1975 just one of the witnesses chose Peter from the police lineup, and that was enough to charge him.

Peter Hain was now in a dark place. He'd been interrogated and the evidence presented to him made him wonder if he'd somehow blacked out and actually committed the crime. But things were about to get darker still. He received a tip (anonymous to this day) that he was being set up by the South African secret police, BOSS. The reason? Revenge – a motive so far-fetched that his legal team advised against mentioning it in court. But BOSS really, really did hate Peter Hain.

In 1969 he'd infuriated the South African Government by hitting their apartheid policy where it hurts... the balls. He had organised mass protests against the Springbok rugby team's tour of the UK, which led to the cancellation of the nation's cricket team tour.

'In South Africa, sport was a religion,' Hain told *The One Show*.

> They used sport to present an image to the world, that they played fair, that sport transcended politics – ignoring, of course, that their teams were 100 per cent white and picked according to the racist policies of the time. The AA campaigns [led by the Anti-Apartheid Movement] really hammered home the hypocrisy to anyone who was in any doubt.

It's safe to say Hain wasn't on the South Africa government's Christmas card list in 1969. But BOSS did send him a present: a letter bomb. 'They'd been sending them to Anti-Apartheid protesters in London,' said Peter. 'Thankfully mine was faulty.' Revenge, BOSS realised, is a dish best served cold.

> They waited a couple of years and framed me for a bank robbery. They found someone who looked vaguely like me, and to make sure that we were both in the same area at the same time, they had surveillance units watching me, who radioed ahead to the robber as I left my house in Putney. I was actually on my way to buy a typewriter ribbon, he was on his way to ruin my life.

Confessions by former BOSS agents later revealed that, after the robbery, Hain's doppelganger was immediately flown out of the country. The plan then was for BOSS to anonymously tip off the police that Peter Hain was a bank robber.

BOSS, though, had reckoned without a group of truanting schoolboys, who witnessed events. They chased after the robber but only one of them, 11-year-old Terry McCann, got close to him.

Terry tells his version of events in a way that only a London cabby can: with an elbow hanging out the window, one eye fixed on the road, the other in the rear view and the meter on:

It was lunchtime and me and three mates were on the High Street – on the other side of the road from the bank. We saw this bloke running, dropping wads of notes and being chased. We started after him too. Pretty soon I was in the front. I got a really good look at him – he's really pegging it. But he just stops and he's knackered, sweat pouring off him. He turns and stares at me, really aggressive like and I got a bit scared, so I turned around. So I went back to find my mates. Minutes later this VW Beetle pulls up and out jumps this student looking geezer – who I now know is Peter Hain. Fresh as a daisy. My mates are going, 'That could be him.' I'm like, 'Don't be stupid, that's a completely different bloke.' Anyway, they take down the number of his car and we follow him into the shop. I'm watching him. He picks up a magazine, he actually says hello to someone he knows and I know that this is not the same man I was just chasing. But the lads I'm with are going, 'Let's tell the manager. We'll get a ride in a police car and the afternoon off school.' I thought they were crazy, this is an innocent man. So I said, 'Nah, I'm going back to school' – which is ironic because I bunked off most afternoons. I thought the police would just know that it was a completely different bloke.

But the police, apparently, didn't. Terry recalls:

The night Peter was positively identified, me and my dad were watching it on the news – it was a big story. I didn't have a clue who *he* was, but he *definitely* wasn't the robber and I told my dad – I was quite excited – and my dad believed me. It was bizarre, because right then the police turn up at our house trying to get me to say that it *was* Peter Hain that I'd seen. My dad knew it was illegal for them to do that and he threw them out. He found out who Peter's lawyer was and phoned him up to tell what I told him.

It wasn't just the police who were trying to get Terry to change his tune. 'I was followed, to and from school. Our house was being watched, we'd get a lot of anonymous phone calls… I still don't know who they were, but they were trying to put the frighteners on me.'

As the Old Bailey trail was announced, Peter Hain's run of bad luck continued. The case was to be presided over by Judge Alan King Hamilton, a cricket fanatic who made no bones of his hatred of Hain for causing the cancellation of the South African team's visit five years previously.

Things began to improve when the witnesses backtracked under cross-examination. All except young Terry McCann.

Described by Hain's legal team as 'a one in a million witness', Terry was the only witness to actually see both the robber and Peter Hain up close within minutes of each other. The evidence of a political plot against Hain – evidence strengthened by the menacing intimidation of the schoolboy Terry – was never brought to play in the trial. Under scrutiny, however, the charge was proved spurious, though not quite ridiculous enough to be thrown out. Matched to Terry's clear-headed account of events, the jury found Hain innocent after six days, clearing the way for a political career that couldn't be mistaken for anybody else's.

WILL THE REAL REGGIE PERRIN STAND UP?

A year before Peter Hain was trying to publicly escape his circumstances, another high-profile British politician was trying to do the same – but this time he was hoisted high by his own petard. In 1974 John Stonehouse was an MP and cabinet minister in Harold Wilson's government. He was, however, facing serious debts from various failed businesses and investments. To avoid multiple bankruptcies he'd also been cooking his books and had come under the spotlight of the parliamentary affairs committee. Now he could add impending fraud charges to his list of woes. Oh, and he was having an affair with his secretary.

Stonehouse's solution was extraordinary. He flew to Florida and faked his own death by leaving his clothes neatly folded on a Miami beach, thus giving the impression he had gone for a terminal dip. In reality, he flew to Australia, where his mistress was waiting.

In Britain the newspapers were already running obituaries, but at the same time in Australia a nervous Englishmen was reported to the police for acting suspiciously in a bank. The bank clerk who made the call told the cops she believed the man to be Lord Lucan, whose recent disappearance was an even bigger story than John Stonehouse's suicide. Bearing no resemblance to Lucan, Stonehouse was nonetheless put under surveillance and later questioned in his new home.

Stonehouse had a fake passport and tried to convince the detectives questioning him that it was all a misunderstanding. But the gig was up when an eagle-eyed detective noticed a book of matches bearing the name of a Florida hotel where a British MP had recently been reported missing, presumed dead.

Extradited back to Britain, Stonehouse was sentenced to seven years for theft and fraud. On his release he was met at the prison gates by his former secretary and mistress. They later married and had a son.

The Stonehouse trial coincided with the first television series of David Nobb's *The Fall and Rise of Reginald Perrin*, in which Reggie famously fakes his suicide by running into the sea. Many think that Nobbs was inspired to write this sequence by the Stonehouse affair. In fact he'd written it some years earlier in the novel on which the show is based, and Stonehouse may have read it. Either way, the Stonehouse affair popularised the phrase 'doing a Reggie' – i.e. faking one's own death.

Stonehouse finally died in 1988.

But, it turns out, he is the bounder who just keeps on giving. In 2010 it was revealed that Stonehouse had been a spy for the Czech government, reporting on Wilson's cabinet secrets since the 1960s. In total, MI5 revealed, his sideline in treachery earned him around £5,000, paid in annual instalments worth a third of his annual parliamentary salary.

LEARNING CURVES

DO MIND THE BOLLARDS

For years, bottlenecks caused by large crowds of people leaving sports stadiums or concert halls at the same time have been a health and safety nightmare. It's a generally uncomfortable and grumpy squeeze for the participants, and there are also obvious safety issues if there's an emergency. But one British expert has come up with a brilliant – albeit somewhat odd-sounding – solution.

Keith Still is a Professor of Crowd Dynamics at Buckinghamshire New University. His work has helped improve the safety of crowds at venues all over the world. He's developed crowd flow models for mass events across the world, including in the UK for the 2011 royal wedding, but his work is also much in demand when it comes to keeping crowds safe in purpose-built, and therefore confined, stadiums and arenas. 'One of the main problems with crowd safety is that many venues have been designed in a way that makes it difficult for crowds to move through the space easily, and then people tend to "jam". Parts of the system just come to a standstill.'

Professor Still's quest began by looking at the work of

American academic Dr John Fruin. In the 1970s Fruin pioneered the study of how groups of people move and interact. But his work focused on the behaviour of *pedestrians* on the street, not the behaviour of crowds in confined spaces like stadiums. 'Crowds move differently to individual pedestrians,' says Keith. 'It may seem obvious, but this wasn't a principle considered when stadia were first designed.'

Exit routes and buildings for use by large numbers of bodies have been designed based on the assumption that people in crowds flow like grains of sand in an egg timer – the people in the middle should move faster. This is called the Poiseuille flow, named after French physicist Jean Léonard Marie Poiseuille, who published his findings in 1839. But crowds aren't grains of sand, they're people, says Professor Still. 'Restrict movement at entrances and gateways, and a semi-circle builds up at the door and that increases the density and crush to get through. Eventually the whole crowd will come to a standstill.'

The realisation that the egg timer model was wrong came to Professor Still when he thought he was off duty. 'Twenty or so years ago, I was standing in the queue at Wembley for the Freddie Mercury Aids Awareness concert... we were in the middle of the crowd and that's where the grains move fastest in an egg timer. But in this real environment the crowds were moving fast around the edges, completely the opposite dynamic to what you would have expected.' So Keith started to question the established dogma on crowds. 'The more I dug into it, the less happy I was with how we were actually modelling crowds.'

Keith had to rethink completely how we get people into and out of stadiums, and, almost against all logic, the solution he came up with involved putting *something in the way of the exit*.

Obstacles in the path of crowds – a bollard, for instance – will actually speed them up.

Keith's research is based on the science of anti-chaos theory, where a chaotic system can become more ordered by small changes to the environment.

So if, for example, we have a doorway and we're trying to get people through the doorway, they'll end up blocking the exit with nowhere to go – which, worst case scenario, leads to very dangerous crushes. Whereas if we put a barrier in the way of the doorway, it forces one mass of people into two groups, we reduce the interactions between people, they'll filter through more easily, and they won't get jammed up.

EVEN MORE BOLLARDS

They're so ubiquitous on British streets we hardly give them a second thought. But the origins of the modern bollard are – honestly – interesting. Especially that distinctive cannon shape, because that's exactly what early bollards were – decommissioned Napoleonic War cannons. These were either the enemy's cannons that had been captured at sea (and which were a different shape and could not therefore be fitted onto British ships) or our own old cannons that were of no further military use. Either way, after the war on the continent was over, tons of iron cannons were sold off as scrap by the Ordnance Board. (Smaller, more expensive, brass cannons tended to be re-smelted or kept as souvenirs.)

Cannon bollards repurposed as street furniture in Southwark and the East End of London are often explained to have been French ordnance captured at the Battle of Trafalgar in 1805. But Martin H. Evans, a historian who is pretty much the definitive voice in the world of repurposed cannons (to be honest, it's a pretty niche area), has exhaustively researched the ships from which they were supposed to have been seized and concluded the story was an urban myth. At first, scrapped cannons were buried muzzle down into the pavements, but London started a trend of setting the guns muzzle up with a real cannonball soldered on top for decorative effect. Hundreds of these originals are located on streets all over Britain.

Of course, actual cannons were a finite resource, leading to the rise of a far less attractive type of bollard appearing on the High Street almost overnight. Though the old iconic cannon shape continues to be used, these new designs were usually angular and made of concrete. In the early 1990s, Britain, perhaps as a consequence of the economic meltdown, was gripped by a scourge of violent robberies – ram-raids, in which thieves would crash stolen cars into the windows of retail stores and make off with the displayed goods. A solution was to position bollards a few feet from the plate glass windows of high-value shops; the negative flip side of this is that High Streets began to resemble the checkpoints of militarily occupied zones – and made for a rather depressing shopping excursion.

THE EYES HAVE IT

If you want to nudge people into acting honestly when they're unobserved, you don't need to splash out on an expensive CCTV system. Instead, simply pin a picture of a pair of eyes on a wall. 'I used to be in charge of the tea and coffee supplies in this tea room at work and I had a problem because people weren't putting enough money in this honesty box to cover my costs,' says Dr Melissa Bateson at the University of Newcastle.

Determined to get her collegues to stump up, Dr Bateson, a behavioural biologist, decided to find out if people's behaviour could be engineered. Could she draw on evolutionary theory to make her workmates pay up? 'The idea was to see if we could use pictures of eyes to alter people's behaviour. Our hypothesis was that eyes might give people a subtle feeling of being watched by others and they might give more money.'

For ten weeks she alternately put up a picture of eyes one week and then a picture of flowers in alternate weeks. 'Amazingly we got nearly three times as much money in the weeks when we had pictures of eyes on the wall compared to the weeks when we had the flowers up.'

It's thought that a primal instinct might be the reason a photograph of a pair of eyes makes us more honest. We are an innately social species and few of us want to risk being cast out of the social group. So even a subconscious fear that we're being watched is enough to keep our behaviour in check.

People are beginning to explore whether this could have real-world applications. One of the first to jump on board was the security department at Newcastle University, where the research first began. For a couple of semesters Ken Nott of the University's Estate and Security Service – the campus cops – had been concerned about the number of bike thefts. 'We identified three specific areas where the pedal cycle thefts were quite high and we put the eye signage in those areas. To our surprise over the six-month trial period the thefts actually decreased.'

BIRD BRAINS?

For centuries the corvids – the family of birds which contains ravens, rooks and crows – have been steeped in superstition and were said to carry the souls of the dead to the afterlife.

Given its gruesome past, the Tower of London is a now fitting home for the largest member of the crow family, ravens.

These highly inquisitive creatures are certainly smarter than your average bird, but lately they've learnt a new trick, which has been catching the yeoman's attention and adds weight to a remarkable claim that corvid intelligence could rival that of the great apes.

The ravenmaster at the Tower is Chris Skaife. 'Ravens have a history of being thieves,' he says. 'They'll steal absolutely anything. In fact one of them recently stole a purse, and proceeded to bury the coins around the tower. They'll take crisps and, if they don't like the flavour, then they'll go and wash it in their bowls to get the flavour off.'

Even more attractive than shiny stuff, as far as the ravens are concerned, is the delicious tourist food. The ravens know where to find the best pickings – the bins. But there was a problem; they're too big to jump inside and reach the food at the bottom. But, to the amazement of Chris and his fellow yeomen, they've taught themselves how to secure the bin's liner with their feet and then hoist it up with their beak, inches at a time until the once unreachable tasty snack is delivered. While it appears to be a relatively new innovation, it's not exclusive to the birds at the Tower: ravens, rooks and crows have been observed doing this all over the UK.

Despite the mess these birds are making, many experts believe it proves that corvids are, in fact, bird geniuses. At Cambridge University, Professor Nicky Clayton, an expert in animal behaviour, has been testing the intelligence of rooks and jays. 'These are not normal tool users in the wild,' explains Professor Clayton, 'and yet give them a problem to solve – in this case using bin liner as a tool to get food that would be otherwise out of beak reach – and they can do it. Just like that, they figure it out.' But even more impressive than being able to innovate and use a tool is the time it takes for them to achieve their goal. 'They pull up the bin liner with their beak multiple times before they get a piece of food, so they're doing a lot of action before they ever get a reward.' What Professor Clayton means is that the bird is thinking into the future. 'Tool use and the ability to think several steps ahead for a delayed gratification, illustrates extraordinary intelligence, and places the corvids in a very exclusive group of clever animals.'

Nicky and her colleagues have devised their own test on jays – and if it sounds similar to a certain ancient fable about a thirsty crow by Aesop, well, that's because it's a known behaviour of our corvid friends and has been observed by humans for thousands of years. In the modern experiment, jays were presented with a tall test tube half-full of water, with juicy wax worms floating just out of reach. Small stones and balls of cork were the only tools provided. The jays quickly learnt that stones raised the level of the water while the cork simply floated on top. 'Understanding that solids displace liquid is a complicated concept that even five-year-old children struggle with.' Nicky believes that this remarkable ability to solve problems bears many similarities to the evolution of intelligence in apes. 'The crow family have huge brains for their body size. They are also long lived like the apes [the oldest known captive crow lived to the age of 59], they are highly social and are brilliant at these physical problem-solving skills. Exactly the same features which have been suggested to be so important in the evolution of chimpanzee intelligence and, in fact, primates in general.'

So the term 'bird brain' may prove to be a wholly inaccurate insult. Their ability to cooperate with one another and use tools to find food suggests that members of the crow family are amongst the brainiest of all animals

It's not just corvids who benefit from social learning, though. Blue tits are pretty sharp, too (and we're not talking about their beaks) – it's just that in modern times we rarely get to see them in action.

Once it was common to see a blue tit pecking the silver foil top of milk bottles for a stealthy slurp of the cream below. Now it's a bit of a folk memory. A shame because it makes redundant a hard-won avian skillset.

Britain has had a long – but now dwindling – tradition of doorstep milk deliveries. Before the Second World War, milk was delivered uncapped. Garden birds – in the main, blue tits – soon developed a taste for the cream that settled at the top.

Birds are lactose intolerant, but blue tits liked cream so much that over a number of bird generations they underwent a Darwinian process of selection so that their digestive systems adapted. In the 1920s, wax-covered cardboard caps were placed on milk bottles, but a 1921 observation proved that the birds in Swaythling near Southampton had learnt how to pick these off. It was a practice that would spread into all of the southern counties within a few years.

In the early 1950s, when post-war aluminium prices fell, milk bottles sported metal caps (colour-coded to designate the cream content of the milk). Aluminium is far more hygienic than cardboard, and easier to penetrate if you have a sharp little beak. By the mid-1950s blue tit populations across the UK had acquired this skill – a fascinating example of social learning. Initially it was a minor inconvenience to customers and milkmen alike, but Britain quickly became endeared to the antics of the opportunistic little blighters.

Why did blue tits acquire this skill and not their common garden counterparts, robins? Robins are clever but extremely territorial. They have been known to copy blue tits, but if a robin wanted to explore the potential of a milk bottle in another robin's patch it would be chased away – not giving the little redbreast enough time to learn how to get at the cream. Blue tits are highly social, share their territories and thus pass their knowledge on to each other. Birds that flock together, then, learn faster and increase their chances to evolve and survive.

MEDICAL CURIOS

A LIFE THROUGH A LENS

Taking to the skies during the Second World War, Flight Lieutenant Gordon Cleaver unintentionally flew into medical history books – by forgetting his goggles.

Cleaver was a Hurricane pilot with the RAF's 601 Squadron and by 1940 already had seven confirmed enemy 'kills'. But like all fighter pilots at the time he knew it would be folly to rest on his laurels. Each time he was scrambled against enemy fighters could easily be his last. Survival in air battle was all about offsetting necessary risk-taking against minute attention to detail. On 15 August 1940, at the height of the Battle of Britain and with Winchester below him, Cleaver must have loudly cursed his forgetfulness as he reached to pull his goggles over his eyes. An enemy fighter – a Messerschmitt ME 109 or 110, according to varying accounts – swooped into range and engaged him in a dogfight. Cannon fire from the enemy plane shattered the canopy of the Hurricane's cockpit and sent splinters of Perspex into Cleaver's unprotected eyes. Blinded in one eye and wounded in the other by the shards of Perspex, the pilot still managed to roll the Hurricane 180° and keep it steady enough for him to bail out.

He was treated by surgeon Harold Ridley at Moorfields Eye Hospital in London, and it took 17 separate operations over a number of years to save Cleaver's second eye. During these painstaking procedures to save Cleaver's sight, Dr Ridley made an observation that would go on to save the sight of countless others.

Normally a healthy immune system will attack a foreign body – in this case a splinter – and any bacteria that has come with it. The area should become inflamed and swollen, rejecting the object and preventing it from doing even more harm. But to Ridley's fascination, the Perspex was tolerated by the body. This intrigued the eye surgeon because he now saw a solution to one of the most taxing yet most common problems in ophthalmology: how to save eyesight after a cataract has been removed.

A cataract is a region of dead cells within the lens of the eye, which most frequently occurs in late middle age. The lens becomes 'fogged up' and that, in turn, causes poor vision and in some cases blindness. In skilled hands, it's straightforward enough to remove a cataract. The issue was what to use to replace the lens. There was no answer. In the nineteenth century, many doctors tried replacing damaged human eye lenses with glass. The trouble was that the immune system attacked the glass as a foreign object, and the operations often ended in disaster.

And then Harold Ridley observed that Perspex seemed to be benign. Even after Gordon Cleaver's long series of operations, tiny shards of Perspex still remained embedded in his eye. Even after years, his eye did not reject the foreign body. For Ridley, it was a eureka moment – albeit slightly protracted.

In November 1949, and after years of research and development, Ridley became the first surgeon to successfully implant an artificial lens – called an intraocular lens – in a human eye. The pioneering operation took place at St. Thomas' Hospital in London. It's no exaggeration to say that Harold Ridley revolutionised ophthalmology. But his initial success at St Thomas' was greeted with fury and even ridicule by many of his contemporaries.

Dr Ridley's son Nicholas remembers his father's disappointment well. 'He thought that his professional colleagues would embrace this new idea. But in Britain at that time the maxim was that you should take foreign bodies out of the eye, you shouldn't be implanting anything into them.'

In the United States it was a different story, and the profession was much more open to innovation. From 1952, Ridley would fly to the USA at weekends to operate there. But, Nicholas explains, his father remained determined for his innovation to spread. 'He only charged his normal fees for operating and he insisted that the process and indeed the inter-ocular lens itself should not be patented; he wasn't interested in money he wanted to try and help humanity.'

It took until 1981 for the US authorities to declare cataract operations safe and the procedure finally became established in the UK towards the end of the 1980s. Today the operation to correct cataracts is one of the most common carried out by the NHS, with roughly 300,000 procedures taking place a year.

The operation is pretty simple. (If, that is, you're a fully qualified ophthalmologist leading a team of highly experienced medical professionals. Please don't try and fix granny's eyes on the cheap at home, especially as you can get it for free on the NHS.) An ultrasound probe is pushed into your cornea and then emits ultra-high frequency sound waves that smash the old cataract-afflicted lens into pieces. Those bits are liquefied and then sucked out, which leaves a capsule shape – which would have held the natural lens in place. The new artificial lens is carefully folded and then injected through the cut in the cornea to unfurl into the vacuum left by the old lens. Ridley himself had both his lenses replaced after developing cataracts in the 1980s. 'I am the only man to have invented his own operation,' he said.

Harold Ridley was knighted for his services to medicine in 2000, his revolutionary procedure having become one of the most commonplace surgical interventions in the world. It is reckoned to have saved the sight of more than 200 million people.

'I think in the end,' says Nicholas Ridley, 'before he died in 2001, he realised that at last he had achieved what he had set out to, and I think he felt that was his contribution to mankind. Needless to say, I am very proud of him for it.'

Squadron Leader Cleaver was grounded after that encounter with the Messerschmitt but kept his rank and stayed with the RAF. He was awarded the Distinguished Flying Cross. Before the war, he had been a well-known skier and in 1931 won the inaugural Hahnenkamm race – the toughest skiing race there is, held annually in Kitzbühel, in Austria. He died in 1994 (not before having an actual cataract operation on his left eye in 1991), and in 2006 the race organisers announced a new trophy in his honour, the Cleaver Cup, awarded to the highest-placed British competitor.

COLD CAMP: THE COMMON COLD UNIT

In 1946, with the Second World War over, the next job was to rebuild Britain. Although the nation deserved a break, few were going to get a proper one. Money was tight and pretty much everything that was rationed during the conflict was still on the restricted list. Holiday camps were big business before the war – and would peak in popularity in the 1950s – but for the moment even they were off limits since most had been requisitioned by the Armed Forces or were being used to house refugees. Some were even taken over by squatters, families who had lost their homes in the Blitz.

But one holiday camp, 3.2 km (2 miles) south of Salisbury, promised guests an all-expenses paid retreat with a glimpse of luxury. Heavenly – just as long as they didn't mind having a runny nose.

This was no Butlin's. It's true that hot meals were delivered to your door, and the latest in entertainment was laid on, too. But not quite so entertaining were the mucus weigh-ins and the injections. There were no Red Coats, only men in white coats; this was Cold Camp.

The study of virology – especially how to cure the common cold – was made a top priority by the government in the 1940s. The utilitarian-sounding Common Cold Research Unit (CCRU) was established on the site of the former Harvard Military Hospital near Salisbury in 1946. This 'pop-up' town of prefabricated huts had been built with contributions from Harvard Medical School (hence the name) and stuffed with boffins studying how to combat anticipated outbreaks of disease such as cholera, which many feared would come after the carpet bombing of British cities. By 1942, with the tide of the war slowly turning, that research was shut down and the campus was taken over by the US Army, which renamed the facility the First United States Army Medical Laboratory. It was here that huge quantities of blood were assembled and catalogued by type in readiness to treat the wounded in the forthcoming D-Day invasion. When the civilian CCRU took over the site, the British medics renamed it Harvard Hospital and established it as a unique institution with a single mission: to rid the nation of the sniffles, or to at least understand them.

What the Unit needed most was volunteers – lots of them – so they hit upon a clever marketing plan to turn catching a cold into a ten-day holiday. They also offered free meals and pocket money, which by the 1970s was approximately 35p a day (£3.80 today). More than 1,200 people from across the UK and from all backgrounds volunteered in the first years of the camp's opening, and throughout its history an average of thirty people would come and stay every ten days.

The holidaymakers were well looked after and many commented on how much they liked the staff. Visitors had private rooms and meals delivered to them, and there was plenty of opportunity for walks in the surrounding countryside and recreational activities. The business side of things – catching a cold – wasn't painful, but nor was it particularly pleasant. Patients had to lie on beds with their heads held back as a doctor or nurse squirted a liquid that contained a cold virus taken from another patient. Your chances of catching a cold were roughly one in three.

Sir Christopher Andrewes (sic) was a founder of the Unit and his son, John, was a human guinea pig there on three occasions between 1946 and 1948. John, now a retired medical doctor, explains:

> My father worked on isolating the first human influenza virus in the 1930s and continued his virology work, culturing the cold virus at Harvard Hospital. I was a student at Cambridge and becoming a guinea pig was a great way of making some extra cash. Of course there were examinations, urinalysis, nasal washes and even X-rays, but it was a strangely tranquil place. Mostly I just remember waiting for the meal cart to come round with dinner or going on long walks.

With ten days to relax and unwind, a young man's thoughts were bound to turn to love. And although men and women were segregated once trials began, John, along with his willing accomplice David, came up with an ingenious way to overcome this obstacle to romance.

'In the meeting before we were isolated, there were two girls in particular, one of whom had recognised me from a previous visit to the Unit. We got the telephone receptionist to connect our telephones and then in the evenings we would chat to these two girls over the phone.' Later John and David would go on holiday in the Lake District with the girls, and although all married different people they remained good friends.

For Lorna Aldridge, the Cold Camp became home. She moved to the site in 1977 with her husband Colin, who took a job as a handyman. 'We'd lost the mortgage on our house in southeast London,' remembers Lorna. 'When Colin accepted the job, we only planned to stay for a couple of months, just to get back on our feet, but we ended up staying for 13 years. We brought up our two children there.' Lorna makes life there sound idyllic. 'It was wonderful. We had 15 acres of land, rabbits in the garden and our children could run around safe and free. It was like another world, such a contrast to southeast London – a whole community complete with post office and shop.'

There was something wonderfully eccentric about the ramshackle Cold Camp, with characters on the staff like Audrey Rogers, who would issue 'campers' with wellies and order them on long, isolated, walks in the countryside to keep fit. Or Keith Thomson, who joined as an administrator after being demobilised in 1946 and ended up being jack-of-all-trades there for 40 years. 'Everyone really cared about the place and I think that's why people kept coming back time and again,' says Lorna. 'One couple even came 22 times, and another actually came on their honeymoon.'

One of Lorna's jobs was to collect and weigh the small bags in which people had deposited their tissues. Not the most glamorous job on the camp but, like John Andrewes, she observed while out on her rounds that love is the strongest virus of all.

There was one couple that actually really liked each other but they weren't in the same accommodation and had to be kept 9 m [30 ft] apart. To make sure they kept their distance they had a piece of string that was 9 m long as a measure, and they both had to hold either end... I understand they may have got themselves tied up around a tree, which brought them face to face – or so I heard.

By 1956 the Unit had discovered the rhino and corona strands for the common cold. Typically rhinoviruses are responsible for around 30 per cent of common colds and the rest are the result of coronaviruses. More than 200 strains are implicated in the cause of the common cold, and over 100 of these were discovered by researchers at the Unit. They also identified that interferon proteins could help prevent infection during the virus's incubation phase, but unfortunately no practical treatment could be developed.

The Unit ran for more than 40 years, and while they never found a cure for the common cold, the scientists greatly improved our understanding of the way colds are transmitted, and how they continually mutate – which, annoyingly, is why a cure is so elusive in the first place. Lifelong bonds are often forged when people are thrown together in adversity, but who could have predicted that nasal swabs and mucus weigh-ins could evoke such memories and be the beginning of such lasting friendships? That's certainly not something to be sniffed at.

THE DOCTOR WILL SURPRISE YOU NOW

Medical school in the nineteenth century really was a boy's only club. But that didn't stop one determined woman revolutionising surgery. She did have to change her name to James, though.

History records Bristolian Dr Elizabeth Blackwell as Britain's first female medical doctor. History is wrong. That 'first' should be bestowed on Margaret Ann Bulkley, who qualified and started practising as a surgeon in 1813 – 40 years before Blackwell. Dr Blackwell gets the credit for good reason, though. Until recently, only the army and a select handful of others knew that Bulkley was a woman.

Margaret became James as a teenager, when her mother, in on the ruse, put her through medical school in Edinburgh. Graduating as Dr Surgeon James Barry, she was an innovative pioneer of nineteenth-century medicine and the first surgeon to successfully carry out a caesarean section. As an army medical officer she served on three frontlines on three continents, implementing new methods of hygiene, sanitation, quarantine, diet and effective treatment of some of the most virulent diseases known to the age. Her medical reforms saved the lives of thousands of people.

But to those who didn't know her secret – which was *everyone* bar her servant who was also, probably, her lover – Barry was a difficult and belligerent man. He made a bitter personal enemy of Florence Nightingale and killed a man in a duel; his elaborate dress sense sparked rumours that he was gay, as did his 'squeaking voice and mincing manner' (as described by the daughter of a foreign diplomat who had once dined with Barry). He was also an evangelical vegetarian.

It was a charwoman hired to prepare the body after his death who discovered that James was actually Margaret. Stretch marks also suggested that Barry had given birth at some point. Although there were some rumours briefly circulating in the press, the army banned a post-mortem and refused to acknowledge the matter.

In 2008, letters written by Barry were compared to those written by a young Margaret and were proved by Alison Reboul, a document analysis expert with the Forensic Science Service, to be of the same hand. Margaret is buried in Kensal Green cemetery as 'James Barry, Inspector of Hospitals', but perhaps it is time Margaret's austere gravestone is recut to give her credit for her remarkable achievements.

THE BONES IN BEN FRANKLIN'S BASEMENT

In November 1997, during renovation work in the basement of 36 Craven Street, an elegant Georgian town house in the very heart of London, the skeletal remains of at least 28 human bodies, and one sea turtle, were unearthed. Work stopped immediately and the police were called. Could this cellar have been the final resting place for the victims of a serial killer? Just a few years previously, the mass murderers Fred and Rosemary West had shocked the British public. The bodies of several women had been found buried in the basement and grounds of their home in Gloucestershire and between them the couple were charged with 22 counts of murder.

The bones and skulls were investigated by the coroner, who identified a mix of adult and baby remains that had been sawed, drilled and cut with great precision, all of them after death. And they all dated to the mid-eighteenth century. British law has no official statute of limitations for suspicious deaths, but a 200-year-old crime is hard to square with the taxpayer and a police investigation was called off.

But a salacious mystery remained because this wasn't just any town house. 36 Craven Street is the only surviving home of Benjamin Franklin, one of the Founding Fathers of the United States (and a genius inventor, statesman and a wit, too, though never a President, as people sometimes mistakenly think). Before drafting the constitution and signing the declaration of independence, Franklin lived and worked at No. 36 between the late 1750s and early 1770s – the same period to which the bones were dated.

So could the Founding Father of the United States have been

a serial killer? Of course not. But that's not to say he didn't know how the bodies came to be hidden under the flagstones.

As the Colonial Ambassador to the British colony of America, Benjamin Franklin lived and worked in London for nearly 20 years in the eighteenth century. In addition to his diplomatic activities, Franklin pursued his other interests of philosophy and science. He had plenty of time to do so; correspondence between London and America was entirely dependent on the fastest sailing ships, and a trip took at least two weeks each way. This was the Age of Enlightenment, when Europe was making huge and ground-breaking advances in science, and Franklin was right in the thick of it. He publicly demonstrated his early experiments with electricity to visitors at No. 36 – among them some of the most eminent thinkers and scientists of the time.

During the mid-1700s, the house was owned by a widow named Margaret Stevenson and her daughter Polly, and in them Franklin found a surrogate family. But No. 36 had another notable resident – a brilliant young doctor called William Hewson, who married Polly in 1770.

Hewson was no ordinary physician; he was one of the most talented human anatomists of the age and people would pay to learn from him or simply because they were interested. Eventually Hewson installed rows of seats in the yard of Craven Street and opened a school of anatomy. Later that century, renovations turned some of that yard into a basement.

Men like Hewson were involved in pushing the boundaries of modern science and medicine, turning surgery from a trade more associated with butchery into a credible profession based on experimentation, logic and evidence. (It is the legacy of those less skilful times that surgeons are addressed as 'Mr' not 'Dr' to this day.) Hewson was especially interested in the human lymphatic system – a bodily highway used to transport lymph, the infection-busting white blood cells encased in a fluid. But in order to increase his knowledge, Hewson, and his surgical contemporaries, had to step into the shadier fringes of the Age of Enlightenment.

Until the Anatomy Act of 1832, the legal dissection of bodies was severely restricted by British law – and enforceable by transportation, even death. The only legitimate source of bodies was those of men and women executed for murder. Demand for fresh corpses to investigate far outstripped supply, so anatomists were forced to turn to body snatchers – otherwise known as resurrectionists, who scoured graveyards in the dead of night and plundered freshly dug graves.

In the eighteenth century, Craven Street was ideally placed for sourcing fresh – dead – bodies. At one end of the street was Hungerford Dock, where drownings and deaths of unknowns by misadventure were common. In the opposite direction stood the famous Tyburn Gallows, where the final journeys of the recently hanged could easily be diverted for a few shillings. And at the rear of No. 36, on land now occupied by Charing Cross station, was a graveyard.

What or who, though, was the source of the infant bones, some of them miniscule and from foetuses? Even resurrection men had qualms when it came to the bodies of children. Again, Craven Street seems to have been well situated; it might just be a coincidence, but Hewson's nextdoor neighbour was a certain Dr John Leake, a male midwife.

Circumstantial evidence aside, we can say with almost

certainty that Hewson – or, more probably, his assistants – were responsible for burying the dissected human body parts on site. We think we can say this because of the turtle bones found among them, and the tiny silver spheres of mercury still rolling about on them. (Bear with us here.) In 1770 Hewson applied to be a member of the Royal Society. His sponsor? Benjamin Franklin. In order to be accepted by the venerable institute, William proved that animals – not just humans – have a lymphatic system. According to the Royal Society's records, he did this by injecting mercury into the cadaver of a turtle – an operation he would have first rehearsed. Hewson was subsequently accepted into the Royal Society.

The illegal snatching and selling of corpses helped doctors greatly improve their understanding of anatomy and general medicine, and it also allowed them to make significant advances in amputation techniques. Men like Franklin accepted the necessity of this deeply unpleasant activity if it meant that science would benefit.

But this story has a poignant twist. Hewson cut himself while working on a corpse, allowing bacteria from the cadaver to enter his bloodstream. He died of septicaemia. A year later Franklin, who until 1775 still supported the idea that America should remain a colony but with some fundamental changes to the way it governed itself, left London to help establish the United States as an independent nation.

He didn't leave Craven Street completely behind. Franklin invited Hewson's widow Polly and her three children to join him in Philadelphia. By bringing Polly and her children to live near him, Franklin created one of the first truly American families, arriving as they did in the newly independent United

States. Polly was at Ben's bedside when he died – not before he'd encouraged William's eldest son Thomas to pursue a career in medicine. A medical dynasty was born; Dr. Melissa Hewson of Philadelphia is the fifth generation of Hewsons to practise medicine, and is currently studying to be a surgeon. She says:

> As a small child I grew up hearing stories from my grand-father about these amazing men of medicine. Hearing these stories certainly created in me a desire to study in the field of medicine and, I have to say, when I get married I don't think I'll ever be able to change my professional name. Being called 'Dr Hewson' on a daily basis will continue to remind me of how truly amazing it is to bear the Hewson name. The bones at Craven Street are symbolic of a remarkable chapter in medical history. It was macabre, but it was necessary and you cannot emphasise enough the great leaps in medicine, and the lives saved, because of it.

GRAVE MATTERS

The practice of stealing the bodies of the recently deceased in Britain led to a boom in burial technology, offered by undertakers as extras. Most simple was the mortsafe. These iron cages placed over graves became a common feature of cemeteries in the eighteenth century (and are still easy enough to find in church graveyards). Coffin collars were popular in Scotland – a thick iron choker was placed around the neck of the corpse and fixed to the bottom of the coffin. The only way to remove the body would be to hack off the head – which, of course, would devalue the corpse considerably. Patent coffins, reinforced with iron and featuring lids that were spring-loaded from the inside, were almost impossible to open, even with a crowbar. In the 1860s, US patents were filed for coffin torpedoes. These small, custom-made, hair-trigger cannons packed enough ordinance to blow the head off a graverobber who disturbed the hair trigger by forcing a coffin lid. It's no coincidence that the coffin torpedo, and its more dangerous counterpart the grave torpedo (basically a landmine), arrived just as the American Civil War was in full swing. Both medical science and emergency surgical practice was ill-prepared to deal with the slaughter on both sides of the divide, so demand for fresh material for students to practice on was very high. If they could afford it, grieving families would go to great lengths to ensure their loved ones kept hold of some dignity in death. Unsavoury as the practice is to modern sensibilities, it is a fact that the influence of bodysnatchers on medical science is greater than any of the advances made during the American Civil War and later the First World War – the first truly modern wars.

MUSIC OF LIFE

STARS (AND STRIPES) IN THEIR EYES

'The Star Spangled Banner' is quintessentially American, and for more than 100 years it's been played at patriotic events and ceremonies, becoming the official national anthem in 1931. The lyrics are as American as apple pie. Originally a poem called 'Defence of Fort M'Henry', they were written in the early nineteenth century as a strong criticism of Royal Navy bombardments during the War of 1812. But the music they are sung to was composed in 1780, over here in Blighty, as the official song of a famously bawdy eighteenth-century gentlemen's club in London.

John Stafford Smith, the organist and head chorister of Gloucester Cathedral, penned the melody on commission from the Anacreontic Society – a London-based club dedicated to the Ancient Greek poet Anacreon, who specialised in odes to drunkenness and laddish behaviour. The lexicographer Dr Johnson and his biographer Boswell, and the composers Hayden and Purcell were all members. Stafford Smith's brief was to come up with an easy to caterwaul anthem that would

underpin a set of quite saucy lyrics to end a night's hard intellectual boozing.

The melody eventually travelled to the United States and it
was on 14 September 1814 that the version we know today
came into being. As British ships bombarded the American
Fort of McHenry, American lawyer Francis Scott Key was
on a British ship negotiating the release of a prisoner. Seeing
the fort's beleaguered US flag flying throughout the fight, he
was inspired to write a poem, which he set to the tune from
the Anacreontic Society. Having spread from London, it had
become a popular tune in the USA, and Key had already used
it for his 1805 song 'When the Warrior Returns'. Key's poem
included such anti-British lines as 'Their blood has washed
out their foul footsteps' pollution', words that are still sung
to this day.

The United States has done pretty well out of their anthem,
but the same cannot be said for the Anacreontic Society. The
exclusively male club closed in 1792 after a meeting was
attended by the curious Duchess of Devonshire, keen to experience the bawdy customs of the society. Even though she
was tactfully hidden behind a screen, many members of the
club became painfully self-conscious. The thought of their
obscenities being heard by a woman of rank and reputation
was mortifying, and membership haemorrhaged.

HAUNTING MELODIES

Beethoven's Symphony No. 9, completed in 1824, just three
years before his death, was to be his last symphony. Or was it?
Well, not according to a dinner lady called Rosemary Brown

from Balham in south London. The otherwise quiet and unassuming Rosemary claimed to be a musical medium, acting as a supernatural scribe for hundreds of 'new' works written by the long-dead giants of classical music. Hailed and ridiculed in equal measure, Rosemary insisted that all she needed to knock out a concerto in the style of a long dead maestro was a direct line to heaven – an assertion that is open to interpretation. What cannot be disputed, though, is that by the time her soul departed in 2001 she had left behind an extraordinary body of musical scores, some of which were recorded by the leading artists of the 1960s and '70s.

It was in 1964 that Rosemary first came to the attention of BBC news, who ran a short piece about her and a newly discovered Liszt piece. She claimed that Liszt, who by that time had been dead for 78 years, first made contact with her when she was a little girl. After that, she said, he would often manifest to accompany her on shopping trips. Sometimes they would watch television together, but he found the innovation largely 'appalling'. During their get-togethers he would often drop hints that, when she was ready, he would use her to transcribe some new sonatas he'd been working on in the spirit realm. And now, she told the incredulous reporter, he had.

Beethoven – or at least the spirit of him, since he died in Vienna in 1827 – also visited Rosemary at home in Balham and dictated to her Symphonies Nos 10 and 11. 'I was very nervous of Beethoven,' she said at the time, 'he looked very fierce.'

A little later, Liszt got back in touch with Rosemary. So did Chopin (who had gone to his grave in 1849), Schubert (1828) and a host of other composers from the upper echelons – all of them long dead but all of them appearing to Rosemary with unfinished business. 'I find that the composers are often with me,' she told another television crew in the 1970s, 'when I'm doing some of the housework.'

There's no doubting that Rosemary Brown delivered a prolific and varied body of work; much of it was published, performed and recorded by world-renowned artists. But how did she write them? Was she a direct channel for the composers, as she was convinced, or had she unknowingly tapped into her own subconscious talent for creating music?

One thing we do know about Rosemary Brown is that she was, at best, a mediocre pianist. She had had a few piano lessons but showed no signs of any compositional skills. Yet the music scores 'dictated' to her by the likes of Debussy, Grieg, Liszt, Chopin, Stravinsky, Bach, Brahms, Beethoven, Schumann and Rachmaninov and written out in long hand were, apparently, recognizably theirs, and, according to some experts – but certainly not all – just as complex.

Rosemary appeared on television and in the papers with some regularity. She was nearly always, gently, mocked. Yet Brown – a genuinely sweet-natured lady who never attempted to make any money from her claims – intrigued musicologists. The music she channelled bore hallmarks of the composers she claimed to work for – some of them hallmarks that only real experts would notice.

Peter Dorling directed a documentary about her in 1969. He remembers:

The first time the crew and I went round to film her, Rosemary said that she couldn't guarantee anything would happen while we were there. We were all worried because we were using film and it was so expensive. Every ten minutes of film was costing us money, so normally we had to be as careful as we could with what we shot. This time we simply had to keep rolling in the hope something would happen; but then, after a while, she would just start to mutter.

Whatever was going on, Peter couldn't explain – he still can't – but Rosemary certainly seemed to be getting instructions from... elsewhere. 'She would say things like, "Move over Beethoven, you're in the way" and then she would chatter away to herself. She would say things like "Do you mean a sharp there? Or an octave up?" What was interesting was that apparently Beethoven spoke English and was no longer deaf!' Some composers, observed Peter, would simply dictate but 'she said that when Chopin was in the room with her, he would actually take control of her hands and press them onto the keyboard.'

Rosemary briefly became a worldwide sensation after the BBC documentary. There were appearances on prime-time US TV and recordings of her music. She had her doubters, but some of her believers were musicians. Leonard Bernstein, perhaps one of the most famous American composers and conductors of the twentieth century, was convinced by her new Rachmaninov piece. Rosemary, though, was uncomfortable in the spotlight and slipped into relative obscurity, convinced not of her own genius but simply that she'd been happy to help a few ghosts out.

Could these melodies really have come from beyond the grave? Or could it be a latent talent deep in Rosemary's brain that could only come out when she was in a specific state of mind? Professor Geraint Wiggins at Queen Mary University of London is an expert on creativity in the brain. 'There's no doubt Rosemary had an interesting talent. I don't believe she was a fraud, just that perhaps it wasn't a supernatural phenomenon.' With Rosemary no longer around to interview, it's difficult to explain the phenomenon definitively, but it's clear she genuinely believed in her explanation of events and Geraint has a theory why. 'Our brains are attuned to music, a complicated and co-ordinated detailed set of things all happening at once. With Rosemary, I believe she was able to pick up on the individual styles and reproduce components of music. She also probably had a great memory and was able to hear the sound and pull these elements from the music, capturing the very essence of the composers.'

GEORGE FORMBY STICKS IT TO THE MAN!

George Formby, the Lancashire born-and-bred singer-songwriter and comedy star of stage and screen in the 1930s and '40s, was one of the biggest-selling recording artists of the time, and certainly one of the best loved. He also set the template for the biggest pop stars today. That might sound incongruous when you consider the attributes he's famed for – gormless looks, playing innuendo-laden songs on a ukulele and boasting an acting range of about nine inches – but the sum of George's parts equalled a certain sort of daft magic that continues to resonate and charm today. What's more, the private and even political side of the man was as racy and controversial as anyone bothering the charts today. He had records banned by the BBC: 'Blackpool Rock (With My Little Stick Of)' is as double entendre-stuffed as the title suggests, but the Queen Mother adored it, so the song was later given a reprieve. He also had a roving eye and attempted affairs with women whenever his famously formidable wife and manager Beryl wasn't looking. He sang and goofed his way through numerous films, his characters always likeable but downtrodden working-class lads who eventually triumphed and got one over the oppressor. In real life, George it seems, was no different.

During a tour of South Africa in 1946, George witnessed first-hand a domestic government policy that would become enshrined in law within two years: apartheid. Neither George nor Beryl liked what they saw and refused point-blank to play in segregated concert halls. As the tour continued, the anger of the National Party grew, along with criticism by the local press. Things came to a head at the end of one concert, when a young black South African girl climbed on stage to give George a bunch of flowers. Formby picked the tot up and gave her a cuddle. This was deemed outrageous and the final straw. No less than Daniel Francois Malan, the architect of apartheid, phoned Beryl backstage to complain. Her riposte to him is legendary: 'Why don't you p*** off, you horrid little man?' George and Beryl were officially requested to leave the country, but not before George had set a precedent for all those rock and rollers who backed causes in his ukulele-jangling wake.

THE SHRILLING FIELDS

British soldiers in the First World War quickly acclimatised to the cacophony of war. But there was one sound they could never ignore – the whistle that ordered them 'over the top'.

Those chilling tones were almost certainly created by an Acme Thunderer or a Hudson Metropolitan whistle, made by the Acme Whistle Company of Birmingham. They were standard issue during the war – famed for their distinctive tone and surprising volume. It was a shrill fanfare of Metropolitans that broke the early morning silence to announce the commencement of the Somme offensive on 1 July 1916. (Ironically, the name Somme is derived from the Celtic word for tranquility.)

Acme's factory was established in 1870 and it continues to be the world's largest whistle manufacturer. During the war they produced millions of Metropolitans (the officer's choice) and Thunderers (preferred by NCOs and squaddies), which were used to peep orders down the lines.

The whistles were deemed so essential that when the nation's stock of brass ran out in 1915 the government sequestered the entire stock of chocolate presentation tins from the nearby Cadbury's factory and handed it to Hudson's. Some Hudson whistles still exist where you can clearly see parts of the embossed Cadbury's logo on the body.

Hudson Metropolitans were originally developed to replace police rattles but are still referred to as 'over the top' whistles. The Thunderer – which became beloved of football referees – had an equally distinct sound, thanks to the Acme innovation of placing a dried pea in the body of the whistle.

During the war Acme factory workers felt guilt and responsibility that their handiwork signalled the end of so many young lives. 'Acme's founder Joseph Hudson's sons and nephews served on the front,' says Acme's current Managing Director Simon Topman. 'It's poignant to think they would have been following the orders sounded by the whistles that their family was famous for. To this day, the small batches of the whistle we now produce are done so with a genuine twinge of sadness.'

THE BONNIE FOUR

What 'Danny Boy' is to the Irish, 'My Bonnie Lies Over the Ocean' is to those with Scottish genes. Its origins prior to being arranged and published as sheet music by the American Charles E. Pratt in 1881 are not definitively known, but it was already a standard by the time Pratt realised he could claim the royalties.

It's possible that the lyrics were in support of Bonnie Prince Charlie (Charles Edward Stuart), who was on the run after his defeat at the Battle of Culloden in 1746. Its lyrics are ambiguous and open to interpretation: *bonnie* is a term of endearment that can be applied to a male or a female, so to sing it after Culloden would be a good way to show where your true allegiances lay while at the same time offering enough of a get-out clause if you were heard singing it by those hostile to Charlie's cause.

Political or not, it's a simple-to-learn tune and boasts a very catchy chorus. Pratt's sheet arrangement was a huge seller and it became a go-to singalong, and lullaby, in households across the world. It also, arguably, became the opening salvo of the music revolution of the 1960s. With its title shortened, 'My Bonnie' was the Beatles' first credited single – albeit as a backing band for singer Tony Sheridan, while they were living in Germany.

Back in 1961, Sheridan was a hotly tipped rock and roll contender (from Leicester, as it happens), cutting his teeth in the nightclubs of Hamburg's Reeperbahn. Playing the same clubs, but much further down the bill, were the Beatles. This was their second tour of duty playing the entertainment sweatshops of Hamburg. They'd lost one member – Stuart Sutcliffe – and their drummer was still Pete Best, yet to be usurped by Ringo Starr, who was also playing the same clubs with Rory Storm and the Hurricanes.

Although they were playing similar material and had even become good friends, Sheridan stood apart from the Beatles because *he* had a record deal – with Polydor – and *they* were still a bunch of unsigned chancers. Sheridan's A&R man Bert Kaempfert was keen to get his signing into the studio as soon as possible. But Sheridan didn't have a backing band; he usually just played solo or with pick-up groups assembled on the night. It didn't take much persuasion to get the Beatles to come along to the studio (actually an empty school hall with some recording equipment) and in a couple of hours they'd cut a frantic version of 'My Bonnie' and half a dozen other tracks.

'My Bonnie' was released as a single by Polydor and went on reach the Top Five in the German hit parade. Polydor insisted that the backing band be renamed the Beat Brothers because, to their ears, 'Beatles' sounded not unlike the German word *pidels*, slang for 'penises'.

The record, while not outstanding, has an infectious back-beat (after a start that sounds more like an Elvis ballad) and features a phenomenal guitar solo in the middle. It was played by Sheridan, not George Harrison (as many think), and is vigorously driven by a group clearly having a whale of a time. Better still, they'd actually got paid for it. Months later, back in Liverpool, repeated requests from customers for an import copy of 'My Bonnie' would eventually draw the attention of record shop proprietor – and future Fab Four manager – Brian Epstein, but for now the band, like Bonnie, 'lay over the ocean'.

SDRAWKCAB SELTAEB EHT

Back-masking is the technique of playing the recording of an instrument or vocals backwards in a forward-playing song. The effect is all over *Revolver*, the Beatles' seventh studio album released in 1966, particularly on 'I'm Only Sleeping' and 'Tomorrow Never Knows'.

But the band first introduced (or as it turns out unwittingly reintroduced) the effect on the song 'Rain', the brilliant B-side of the single 'Paperback Writer'. The story goes that having, er, accidentally puffed on something that's probably illegal, John Lennon put the master tape of 'Rain' on a reel-to-reel player the wrong way around, so it played in reverse. The next day he repeated the process for the rest of the band, who lobbied George Martin to incorporate the effect somehow into the song.

That was John's version of events. But the pre-Beatles career of their legendary producer George Martin included experimenting with sound effects for scores of comedy records and he almost certainly knew that Lennon had chanced on exactly the same spooky, otherworldly audio effect that Thomas Edison discovered when he invented recording some hundred years earlier. Edison was as aurally enamoured as John when he accidentally played a wax-recorded cylinder in reverse. He wrote, 'The song is still melodious in many cases, and some of the strains are sweet and novel, but altogether different from the song reproduced in the right way.'

And even before that Mozart composed the 'Mirror Duet', whereby two musicians perform the same piece of music… only one of them is reading it upside down and backwards.

What Mozart and later Edison and even later Lennon hit on was that melodies played backwards can, sometimes, be as attractive as forwards. That sounds obvious, but is in fact quite often down to chance – the chance that the structure, rhythms and distribution of the notes played backwards have a magical symmetry. Take 'Don't Stop' by the Stone Roses on their debut album. This is almost entirely the preceding track – 'Waterfall' – backwards. And thanks to kismet it becomes one of the album's high points. But a lot of the time accidental back-masking, even though it's meant to sound out-there and organic and just, kind of, 'Wow man"' actually sounds like the freeform jazz noodlings of a maniac. Backwards. And nobody wants that. So to get a back-masking effect that's completely guaranteed to work, it needs to be deliberately composed. Backwards.

Beatles expert Andre Barreau explains:

The solo on 'I'm Only Sleeping' is composed backwards, deliberately, meaning George Harrison, instead of just playing randomly and saying that sounds nice… chose and composed it in a melodic line but backwards. That is an arduous process whoever does it. That was a six- or seven-hour session, apparently. Geoff Emerick, who was the chief engineer at the time, said that it was a very long and frustrating day. My take on it is I'm really pleased George Harrison took the time, we've ended up with a beautiful piece of music.

Back-masking isn't just about enhancing a song. It's been used by bands – not least the Beatles – to plant 'Easter egg' messages for their fans deep within the grooves of their records. When played normally, the message will sound like gibberish, but when the song is played in reverse the original message can be heard, if you listen really… really… shhh… carefully. Usually these are completely benign studio in-jokes. But some people read sinister purposes into the practice, and others say that they pick up subliminal orders from the messages. The backwards chatter on 'Revolution 9' from *The Beatles* (also known as the *White Album*) is, reportedly, 'Turn me on, dead man', which sparked the notorious Paul is Dead urban myth. Actually it is a looped recording of an engineer saying 'Number Nine'. Interestingly the British Satanist and occultist Aleister Crowley – once dubbed no less than the 'wickedest man in the world' – wrote at the turn of the twentieth century that trainees of magic would benefit from listening to records backwards. Crowley's photograph is featured on the cover of the Beatle's 1967 magnum opus *Sgt. Pepper's Lonely Hearts Club Band* – he's second left in the back row, next to Mae West.

Latterly British heavy metal band Judas Priest went through a traumatic court case in the USA, accused of placing Satanic messages in their records, urging fans to kill themselves. The band were found innocent. US rockers Tool readily put their hands up when they were accused of hiding subliminal messages in their hit record 'Intension'. Listening back to them they do sound eerie and a little demonic – as backwards recordings tend to – but the actual message being transmitted could have been commissioned by the right-wing decency groups who want to stamp this sort of thing out: 'Work hard, stay in school.'

GLEE IS THE MAGIC NUMBER

We might associate the word glee with the high camp shenanigans of the hit US TV show *Glee* and the 43 million spin-off albums that were sold off the back of it. Charting the adventures of a US high school choir, it's a quintessentially American show about a quintessentially American phenomenon – Glee Clubs. Except it isn't, because Glee Clubs are actually a British institution, the first recorded during Georgian times. A glee is a type of song, usually upbeat, secular and fun. (In Old English *gleo* means 'jest'.) The songs drew inspiration from Renaissance and Baroque madrigals, and what is really distinct about them is the way the harmonies interweave. As the name suggests, a Glee Club was a group brought together to sing the songs. There were strict rules around the definition of a glee. It was for men only, and it had to be in three, four or five solo parts, unaccompanied by any instruments.

So how did we get from the original Georgian Glees to the glitzy jazz hands type of music we associate with the US TV series today? 'It's entirely an English style of music. The most important development was the foundation of the Noblemen and Gentlemen's Catch Club in London in 1761,' says music historian Brian Robins. 'A very important part of the proceedings apart from the singing was socialising, drinking, eating, and there were no ladies allowed at all.' Glee Clubs had members from the highest echelons of society – and even a future king, George IV. 'They took their singing very seriously, it wasn't just everyone sort of bawling their heads off,' says Brian. Another early Glee Club was founded at Harrow School in 1787, and it's a tradition that's still going strong today in the shape of an annual inter-school competition where the different Harrow houses compete for the 'Glees and Twelves'. David Woodcock, the Director of Music at Harrow, explains, 'The competition for glees and twelves, I think, is probably the most keenly contested competition in the school year. The reason for that is that it's played out in here, with the whole school. The atmosphere is like a tinderbox.'

In the mid-nineteenth century, glees moved across the pond to America. Universities such as Yale and Harvard expanded the genre to include other types of choral singing. But glees were popular outside of academia, branching off into what's now known as barbershop, which in turn would inspire the genre that began on street corners, doo-wop.

INSTRUMENTS OF TORTURE

At the hands of a talented player, the recorder is a musical instrument of great melodic and emotional range. In the hands of anyone else, the recorder is the sound of hell in a hollow stick. So how did it become the first musical instrument most children are allowed to get their mitts on? Once the star of Renaissance music, it was reinvented in the twentieth century as a cheap educational instrument. Carl Orff – the composer responsible for the high drama of *Carmina Burana* – was an advocate of recorder-playing in schools in Germany and the UK. His *Musik für Kinder* features recorder arrangements that are simple for young players with little hands to pick up. But the recorder's widespread use is more to do with economics. First mass-produced in Bakelite, and then cheaper still in plastic, recorders could be bought for a song in bulk by educational authorities, and the apparent ease with which it could be taught meant that between the 1950s and 1990s most households with kids of primary age were subject to screeching renditions of 'London's Burning'. Cheaply produced harmonicas and ukuleles are now more popular. They don't sound much better – unless it's *your* little prodigy playing them, of course.

GET YOUR HOUSE IN ORDER

In 1994 the dance act Orbital made their debut at Glastonbury Festival with a performance that was to become part of musical legend. This was the first time Glastonbury was broadcast live on TV, but it was also the first time that the festival took electronic music seriously – in particular House music and it's harder cousin Acid House. Orbital's unique sound was trailblazing on two fronts – it was heard at a festival more usually associated with rock music and beamed straight into the nation's living rooms, where it's safe to say few people had heard the music that had been making headlines that year.

Acid House had exploded onto the British musical landscape in 1987, changing the music scene forever. At that time it was virtually impossible to get a licence for an all-night event, so the organisers were forced to go underground. Party organisers began to look outside London, where people could dance till dawn, away from the authorities and often accompanied by the new drug ecstasy. The rave was born,

Journalist Scott Manson lived the scene, wrote for *Mixmag* and later became editor of *Ministry*, the magazine from the Ministry of Sound. He explains:

> When Acid House came along it felt, well, it felt like a revolution, but back then it was very egalitarian... you know you had gay, straight, black, white, a student dancing with a gangster. It was a really open-minded situation, it was fabulous... but you had to know where it was all happening.

There was no social media – unless you count payphones and postcards. A mobile phone was something people still stopped and stared at in the street when they saw one being used. You had to be resourceful, remembers Scott, if you wanted to find a rave.

> It was a bit of an adventure and it was sometimes very, very tricky to get there. You'd very often be travelling in convoy, but the problem that could come up would be if you followed the wrong car. Early ravers would often converge on motorway services to get their bearings, and in their own way these gatherings became parties in their own right.

Central to these parties was the London Orbital Motorway, the M25 – opened by Margaret Thatcher in 1986. The dance act Orbital was named after those M25 parties and was created by Paul Hartnoll and his brother Phil. 'We all grew up in the '80s listening to really expensively produced electronic music and loving it,' says Paul, 'and then all of a sudden technology started getting cheaper and cheaper and you could make fairly respectable recordings in a bedroom. Essentially we just started with a drum machine and a synthesizer or two.'

Orbital burst onto a thriving, hugely popular but essentially underground scene in 1989 with the track 'Chime'. But by the early '90s the parties were starting to become a victim of their own success and lost some of their charm when the music industry and criminals began to capitalise on the huge gatherings. And by 1994 the government had had enough and began targeting these illicit gathering.

In an unprecedented act, it passed the Criminal Justice and Public Order Act 1994 to outlaw parties that included any sound 'wholly or predominantly characterised by the emission of a succession of repetitive beats'. Known commonly as the 'repetitive beats act' it was a singularly unpopular piece of legislation but it worked: it gave the police powers of dispersal and arrest for a group of people that numbered more than two, and it killed the rave scene.

That year Orbital debuted at Glastonbury, introducing dance music to one of the rock festival's main stages. Says Paul:

> I used to go to Glastonbury every year and I was always saying, Why is there no dance music on these stages? This was '94 – I had been going since '87. We played after Björk. It was absolutely brilliant. Me and my brother even did a little dance that we used to do as kids at the side of the bath, banging our bums together! Michael Eavis [the founder of the festival] enjoyed it so much that he said, Right, I'm going to set up a dance tent for next year, and it's kind of grown – the entire dance area of Glastonbury – and we all ended up on the main stage before Pulp the year after that."

Following the introduction of the Criminal Justice Act, ravers poured back into the cities, and inside (where they could enjoy their music without fear of judicial reprisal), giving rise to the superclub. At Glastonbury, Orbital's legendary performance paved the way for the opening of the dance village, putting electronic music on the festival map and confirming dance music's crossover into the mainstream.

WE ARE NOT AMUSED

PRINCESS IN PERIL

On the evening of 20 March 1974, Princess Anne and her then husband Captain Mark Phillips were returning to Buckingham Palace in a chauffeured royal limousine, an Austin Princess IV.

Scotland Yard's Royal Protection Squad, A Division, was responsible for protecting the Royal Family. But what happened on that fateful evening would change security procedures and the day-to-day lives of the Family forever.

As the limo made its way along the Mall, it was followed by a black Ford Escort. The car overtook the royal party and stopped, blocking the road ahead. The driver of the Escort was 26-year-old unemployed labourer Ian Ball, and his plan was to kidnap Princess Anne to hold her to ransom.

Ball knew the route the princess was travelling. He later told police that he'd called Buckingham Palace's press office and enquired about her engagements that day –they furnished him with the details, without question.

Ball jumped out of his car and began firing a gun at the limo. Inspector James Beaton, the Princess's personal police officer was sitting in the front passenger seat next to the chauffeur. 'I got out of the passenger seat onto the pavement, with the idea of getting between him and Princess Anne's door. There was this sort of bang and he'd shot me in the shoulder. It was then I realised I better shoot back.'

Bleeding from his wound, Inspector Beaton reached into his jacket for his shoulder holstered gun – a Walther PPK. (These were standard issue for close-protection officers but were also famous as James Bond's firearm of choice.) 'I fired a shot that I thought was in his direction but I obviously missed. I tried again and it jammed,' remembers Beaton. Ball was bearing down on the policeman, 'He said, "Put your gun down... put your gun down or I'll fire" and I thought, "Well, it makes no difference anyway."'

Now unarmed, Beaton saw that his only chance to get between the Princess and Ball was to enter the car from the other side and make himself a human shield.

I scrambled inside, put my hand up in front of the window and he fired. The bullet went into my hand. To me it was either forward or back, so I just kept going forward. I kicked the door open and of course he was standing there and he fired – the shot went into my abdomen.

Princess Anne's chauffeur, Alex Callender, then got out to help Beaton and was shot by Ball. Brian McConnell, a tabloid journalist who happened to be passing, also intervened, and took a bullet to the chest.

Ball was now attempting to drag the Princess out of the car, but she dug her heels in. At that point, Police Constable

Michael Hills arrived; he was also shot, though not before managing to call for police backup.

With the bodies of seriously injured men littering the street, the scene was starting to resemble *Lock, Stock and Two Smoking Barrels* – and chancing into it was a character who would have been well cast in that film. At a neck-craning 1.9 m (6 ft 4 in) former boxer Ron Russell was built like a proverbial brick house. He was driving up the Mall on his way home from work. What caught the patriotic Londoner's eye caused him to slam on the brakes and get involved. (If you read the following quote in Ray Winstone's accent, you'll get a measure of Ron's delivery.)

'I see a police officer approaching the car, running from the Queen Mother's house. And I see him [Ball] turn and shoot the police officer and I thought, "No, that's too strong, that's a liberty, can't be doing that.'

Ron could see Ball was trying to get the Princess out of the car. Pulling up on the kerb Ron steamed into the fray.

> He's got a tug of war going on with Princess Anne; he put the gun right up at her forehead pulling her by the arm. And I went to hit him, then he turned his head away and I hit him on the back of the head. He rose up, he turns and he fires at me. That missed me and hit a taxi coming down the Mall.

This was not a fight that observed the Queensbury rules which govern boxing. 'I get round to the near side, lean into the car. I said, "Come this way, Anne, you'll be safe. Now I'm gonna take you out of here and we're gonna walk away and he's going to have to get through me to get you."'

Ball was not giving up, though. 'At that point Mark Phillips has seen him come round behind me. He grabbed hold of Anne and pulled her back into the car. And I turn and he stood there glaring with the gun. So I hit him on the chin. And down he went.'

When the police searched Ball's car they found a letter addressed to the Queen demanding a ransom of £3 million. They also discovered valium tranquilisers and two pairs of handcuffs. At the Old Bailey on 4 April 1974, Ball pleaded guilty to attempted murder and kidnapping. He was sentenced to a life term in a mental health facility, where he remains to this day.

It's still the only attempt to kidnap a member of the British Royal Family.

There were many heroes on that fateful night. Princess Anne visited her bodyguard James Beaton and the other wounded men (all of whom thankfully recovered from their injuries) to say thank you.

James Beaton would help protect the Royal Family for a total of 14 years. And for his courage that March night he received Britain's highest civilian award for bravery, the George Cross. Hills and Russell were awarded the George Medal, and Callender, McConnell and Edmonds were awarded the Queen's Gallantry Medal.

Ron proudly recalls the medal ceremony. 'The Queen, presenting me with the medal, she said: "This medal thanks you from the Queen of England, but I want to thank you as Anne's mother."'

Although it was one of the biggest stories of the year, the exact details and witness testimony pertaining to the kidnapping attempt were subject to a 30-year rule and kept hidden in the National Archives until 2005. In them is an interview with Princess Anne recounting her version of events. She told investigators: 'He had pointed his gun at me and said: "I want you to come with me for a day or two, because I want two million. Will you get out of the car?" 'I replied curtly: 'Not bloody likely – and I haven't got two million."'

At the top of the report is a note, hand-written in green ink by then Prime Minister Harold Wilson, which reads: 'A very good story! It's a pity the Palace can't let it come out.'

THE KICK-ASS QUEEN

In September 2015 Queen Elizabeth II smashed her great-great-grandmother's record as Britain's longest-reigning monarch. It's quite an achievement and it's been quite a reign, but Elizabeth would do well to remember she's had a much less danger-ous ride than Great-Great-Granny. Victoria's long tenure was punctuated by not one but eight assassination attempts – all of them foiled, pretty much by dumb luck.

Had just one of that octet of deadly serious attempts on her life been on target, the course of British history would have changed irrevocably. Fortunately for the Queen, however, they were carried out by a veritable platoon of troubled individuals. Among the more interesting were a humpbacked teenager, an army major who suffered a violent change in character every time he saw the colour blue and a poet out for revenge after Buckingham Place snubbed his epic verse.

The Queen is quoted as saying that, 'It is worth being shot at to see how much one is loved.' And she was even issued with her own means of defence – a fashionable parasol with a secret; the silk covered what was basically a collapsible chainmail shield that could deflect a sword swipe. But even so, she perhaps should have invested in better – at least smarter – security.

One would-be assassin, John Francis, attempted to shoot Queen Victoria as she passed through Constitution Hill in 1842. He missed and managed to escape. The next day he tried to shoot her again; this time practically on her doorstep. A policeman named Trounce had been on royal protection duties at Constitution Hill and actually recognised Francis when he fetched up, armed, at Buckingham Palace. But Trounce was so torn between his loyalty to tradition and his duty to protect the Queen that rather than take down the potential murderer of an Empress by any means necessary… he stood to attention and saluted the passing carriage. John Francis got his shot off but, fortunately, it missed and he was arrested.

Some 40 years later, Roderick Maclean, angry because the reams of poetry he'd sent to Buckingham Palace for review had been ignored, decided that the next logical step after failing to be made Poet Laureate would be to kill the Queen. Attempting to do exactly that, he unwittingly exposed a glaring procedural error in Victoria's security. No bodyguards saw Maclean as a threat among the hundreds of faces gathered to cheer the Queen – even if he was waving a gun. That's because they had been previously instructed to keep their eyes on the monarch at all times – not the crowd.

Maclean was tried for high treason, which was first defined in the 1351 Treason Act passed during the reign of Edward III. Basically the charge covers a criminal act or a betrayal against the Crown or State – so an attempted assassination of the Queen would definitely cut it. In past centuries, if you were caught trying to take out a royal and found guilty of high treason, you could expect bloody retribution, and you would be agonisingly conscious for much of that process. First you would be hanged almost to the point of death, then cut down and brought round in order to witness your own disembowelment. Relief would come only when your head was cut off and then your body divided into quarters. The Gunpowder Plotters – who scored a treason double whammy by trying to blow up Parliament *and* King James I in one explosion – were all 'hanged, drawn and quartered' except the most famous of the gang, Guy Fawkes. Anticipating his impending butchery, Fawkes waited until the noose was placed around his neck and threw himself from the scaffold, breaking his neck in the process and thus ensuring a quick death.

By Victoria's reign and Maclean's attempt to end it, high treason was still punishable by death – though, more reasonably, by hanging alone. Maclean was found 'not guilty, but insane' and sentenced to spend the rest of his life in Broadmoor Asylum. The Queen disagreed with the ruling, feeling that even though Maclean *was* mentally ill he was still guilty of the crime. Her complaint led to the Trial of Lunatics Act 1883, which could base the punishment – hospital or prison – on whether the defendant was guilty of a criminal act in spite of or because of their mental health issues. After all, Victoria had been the target of eight attempts on her life by assassins who all suffered from varying mental health conditions, and she hoped that the new ruling might deter future murderous endeavours.

F*** FELIXSTOWE

Disappointingly, and contrary to popular myth, the last words of King George V as he lay dying at Sandringham in 1936 were not 'Bugger Bognor!'. He is supposed to have made his feelings clear in response to an invitation to come and visit the royally approved seaside town when he felt better, but in fact what he actually said was 'God damn you' after a nurse delivered a sedative via a hypodermic needle. Certainly the King was familiar with Bognor; he'd stayed there in 1929 to recuperate following surgery the previous winter. As the story goes — all the more plausible since he was famously gruff – the town's great and the good petitioned George V when he was about to leave, asking him to give it the suffix *Regis*, Latin for 'of the king'. Then, as now, it impresses the tourists and for the locals it's a snooty way of pointing out that 'here' is better than the next town. (A bit like the difference between Tesco Value brand and Tesco Finest.) George's private secretary relayed the request from the town's burghers and the King bluntly responded: 'Bugger Bognor!'. His private secretary took it upon himself to finesse that into something along the lines of 'His Majesty would be absolutely delighted, please proceed'.

Another royal – well, sort of royal – with a beef against British seaside towns was Edward VIII's squeeze, both the nemesis of the Windsors and, perhaps worse, an American, Wallis Simpson.

In 1936 Simpson, who was already in a highly controversial relationship with King Edward VIII, had set a date to divorce her second husband, Ernest Simpson, on the grounds of his, ahem, adultery. She chose the County Court in Ipswich as the venue for the hearing, wagering that events in the sleepy backwater would go unnoticed in the capital. First, though, she had to prove she was a resident in the jurisdiction, so she and two companions moved to nearby Felixstowe for the minimum period of six weeks.

Compared to her highfalutin style in London, life in the sticks was the ultimate drag. Wallis clearly wasn't getting any kickbacks from the local tourist office when she wrote about the town in her memoirs *The Heart Has its Reasons*, published in 1956:

My first impression of the little house in Felixstowe was dismaying. It was tiny, there was barely room for the three of us, plus a cook and a maid, to squeeze into it.... the only sounds were the melancholy boom of the sea breaking on the deserted beach and the rustling of the wind around the shuttered cottages.... No hint of distant concern penetrated Felixstowe. When I walked down to town for the mail and the newspapers not a head turned... on fair days, we used to walk alone on the beach and for all the attention ever paid to us, we could have been in Tasmania.

Wallis's hopes for the case to pass unnoticed in Ipswich on 27 October 1936 were dashed when a tip-off led to the town becoming besieged by journalists and paparazzi from across the world.

The local police didn't make reporting easy that day. They closed off streets around the courts to pedestrians and raided offices overlooking the courts that had been hired by a selection of newspapers: cameras were, allegedly, confiscated.

The hearing lasted 25 minutes and Wallis was granted a

decree nisi by Mr Justice Hawke, who heard from a broad range of witnesses giving evidence of Ernest Simpson's infidelities with a young woman known as Marigold at the Hotel De Paris in Bray-on-Thames. Leaving court and waving 'ta ta' to her beloved Felixstowe, Wallis raced, by car, back to the normality of London. The assembled press gave chase but were delayed – again, by the local police who chose that day, of all days, to spot-check every car leaving the town (bar Mrs Simpson's).

The Ipswich divorce hearing meant Wallis Simpson was free to marry again. It was the catalyst for the Royal Family's biggest constitutional crisis in modern times when Edward VIII abdicated his crown that December in order to marry Mrs Simpson. They wed in June the following year.

LET IT MBE

Compiling the Honours list is a tricky enough business. But what happens if a potential recipient refuses? Or, worse still, accepts – and then sends it back in a fit of pique? In the former they may make political hay. In the latter, the honours are stored away in a highly secure limbo – just in case the recipient changes his mind.

The honours list isn't infallible. It wasn't a coincidence that Harry Corbett (the puppeteer who created Sooty) and Harry H Corbett (actor, best known for *Steptoe and Son*) both received OBEs in the same year. That was a typo that would have been too embarrassing to admit. Nor is the list compiled by psychics; you just can't tell how some people might react. That's why potential recipients of an honour from the Queen are informed privately; it's up to them if they want to make the offer public. Cynical observers of the practice might note that the more 'edgy' the celeb, the more likely they'll denounce the offer via the press.

More controversial is when an honour is accepted – and then returned.

The Indian poet Rabindranath Tagore returned his knighthood in protest against the 1919 Amritsar Massacre. In living memory, the most famous case is that of John Lennon. The Beatles had been made MBEs in 1965, for their services to British exports – amid some controversy. A livid Squadron Leader Paul Pearson dispatched his MBE back to St James Palace, as did Colonel F. W. Wagg, who returned all nine of his distinguished service medals plus three foreign decorations to the Queen.

In 1969 Lennon decided to return his MBE, citing Britain's involvement in Nigeria's civil war. John dispatched his chauffer, Les Anthony, to the Palace with the insignia and a pithy note explaining that in addition he was also protesting against his latest single's failure to chart.

Returns, then as now, are dealt with by the Central Chancery of the Orders of Knighthood at St James's Palace – the department of the Lord Chancellor's Office that administrates the honours list. John Lennon's, in its original box embossed with his name, is still in the vault. The law states that a still-living recipient is welcome to ask for it back anytime. If they are dead, only his immediate next of kin can have it. So far, Yoko hasn't been in touch. But the Liverpool Beatles Appreciation Society has been, asking if the honour could be displayed at John Lennon's childhood home, where his Aunty Mimi originally displayed it on the mantelpiece. The Palace said no.

The medal remains with the Chancery. The irony of ironies is that, unless Squadron Leader Pearson and Colonel F. W. Wragg subsequently went cap in hand to ask for their medals back, all the medals are probably sharing the same drawer.

THE WINDSORS' LAST STAND

In 1940 Hitler's armies swept across Europe and an invasion of Britain seemed inevitable (see Bish! Bash! Bosch! page 51 and Did the Eagle Land? page 199). As a result, secret plans were put into place to protect the Royal Family, but it's only recently that the details of these have come to light.

The files of what was to be known as the Coats Mission reveal a plan to evacuate the royals if the Nazis landed. In charge of ensuring their escape was Major Jimmy Coats of the Coldstream Guards.

First, and most important, the King, Queen and princesses would be moved to a safe house. The location of the safe house was known only to a select few of its officers. One of those in the know was Colonel Malcolm Hancock. Before Colonel Hancock died in 1989, he was interviewed on tape for the records of the Imperial War Museum, which, sadly, have been rarely heard:

. . . if by any chance... the Royal Family had to be evacuated from London for any particular reason, they would be whisked away to any of four country houses which had been selected [by Major Coats] for them to go to and we, the Coats Mission, would go with them and take up the defence of that particular house, up to the last man and the last round.

Captain Hugo Codrington serves with the Coldstream Guards today and has been given access to the Coats files. Escaping the invaders was a well-rehearsed operation.

The Royal protection group would have immediately loaded the Royal Family into their Humber Ironside vehicles, which were quite boxy, quite slow, but very highly armoured and they would have set off with motorbike outriders racing them up to whichever country house had been selected. Simultaneously there would have been the 124 men based at Bushy Park who would have been in buses straightaway, moving up to provide that ring of steal around the selected house.

The beautiful, Grade I listed Newby Hall in Yorkshire was one of the four houses that had been prepared in case the worst should happen, all picked because they could be adequately secured and were already familiar to the Royal Family. 'Each of the four houses had to be made into a local fortress and the work had to be done with the greatest secrecy. It was absolutely vital that as few people knew where they were and we had to be most careful about everything we did or said,' Colonel Hancock told the Imperial War Museum.

Richard Compton is the owner of Newby Hall and the grandson of Edward Compton, its owner during the war. Edward received the order that his house was needed from Sir Ulick Alexander, wartime Keeper of the Privy Purse.

We have documents that show the secret correspondence going on between my grandfather Edward Compton and his head of household Walter Dale. One read: 'You will no doubt have heard from Mrs Compton about the possibility of housing and accommodating a high government official...' That was the first indication that they had that the Royal Family might need to use the house.

In spite of the secrecy, there were some pretty specific requests.

They were told they would have six hours before the 'people arrived' and to get the appropriate rooms ready, and interestingly they were supposed to get some specific foods and drinks ready.... 'Cream Cracker Biscuits, a Ham (to be cold), Chickens and Eggs, etc. can be perhaps be got later as wanted from farm, 12 bottles of Hock or Chablis, 2 medium sherry and 2 bottles of whisky.'

Hock, a German wine, was an interesting choice, but given the circumstances most people would drink anything alcoholic, even if it was unpatriotic.

Whilst making sure the appropriate food and drink was available for the royal party, there were also serious practical changes that had to be made to turn the house into a fortress. And even though these were done with the upmost secrecy, they didn't escape the quick eye of local schoolboy, John Holt, now in his eighties.

I remember a pillbox being made at the entrance to the stables behind the house... where machine gunners would have repelled a direct attack. And whenever you walked around the gardens you could see a lot of rolled-up barbed wire that had been hidden under tarps and the like. They've gone now, but the fields around the house had also had railway sleepers planted deeply and vertically into the grounds and we thought at the time it must have been to stop airplanes from landing.

Did other locals know what was going on? 'It was an open secret,' admits John. 'Everyone in the village knew the big house was being made ready to receive someone important and made ready to defend, but no one would have mentioned it to each other – "Careless talk costs lives" and all that!'

Had the invading army got too close for comfort, the royals would be rushed to Liverpool, put on a waiting ship and taken to Canada.

Newby Hall was on high alert for two years, but code word 'Cromwell' was never to be used; Germany's push into Russia meant that the threat of a British invasion evaporated. Colonel Hancock remained proud of his involvement all the same.

We thought it was a marvellous honour to be chosen to be part of an organisation with that object in view, it was a marvellous thing. All my company was absolutely hand-picked, and there was tremendous competition amongst the guardsmen to get into the Coats Mission Company... And the one objective was that we comport ourselves honourably when it came to doing our job.

GOOD KING BESS?

According to legend (a polite term for conspiracy theory), the ten-year-old Princess Elizabeth, daughter of Henry VIII, was sent to stay at Overcourt, a manor house in the village of Bisley in the Cotswolds. She was to lodge there to escape an outbreak of plague in London, but she soon caught a fever and, within weeks, was dead.

This was an awkward set of circumstances for Lady Kat Ashley and Thomas Parry, Elizabeth's governess and guardian respectively, since their one job was to look after her wellbeing. King Henry VIII was with a hunting party at nearby Berkeley Castle, and now word had arrived that he was on his way to check on things at Overcourt.

Terrified of getting the chop, literally, Ashley, Parry and the squires of Overcourt planned to make a substitution. A pretty, ginger-haired lookalike from the village would be sought, dressed in Elizabeth's clothes and sworn to secrecy. Unfortunately, no girls in Bisley answered that brief, but there was a local boy called Neville who did. Desperate times call for desperate measures and Neville was recruited. Since Henry rarely spent longer than a few curt minutes every few months with the princess, it was hoped he could be relied upon not to notice. Apparently Henry didn't – and nor did anyone else during Neville's lifetime as Elizabeth. With the benefit of hindsight the reason why Queen Elizabeth I never married or had children is now obvious.

Dracula author Bram Stoker popularised the conspiracy of the Bisley Boy in his book *Famous Imposters*. But in the 1970s folklore collector Katherine Briggs found that it was in fact a nineteenth-century ruse by Bisley's vicar, Thomas Keble, to explain the female child bones in an ancient stone coffin at Overcourt during renovations.

Berkeley Castle, by the way, is home to another royal conspiracy theory. It was here, in September 1327 that Edward II was imprisoned and then murdered.

The gruesome, and popular, version of events is that Edward met his fate at the wrong end of a red-hot poker. Edward had already been forced to abdicate – in part because he was, in the context of the times, relatively open about his homosexuality. His mode of dispatch was probably just propaganda to discredit the former King's reputation. In reality, Edward was probably either suffocated in his sleep at Berkeley or died of natural causes sped up by his rapidly diminished circumstances.

THE SNOW QUEEN

December 1981 began mild and balmy before the temperatures suddenly plunged. By 8 December, deep snow had brought chaos to London's roads and railways. A new record for the lowest temperature in England was set on 13 December: -25.2°C (-13.4°F) at Shawbury, Shropshire.

As people across the country struggled to get home, the Cross Hands hotel and pub in Old Sudbury, Gloucestershire, had more than 100 desperate travellers seeking refuge from the heavy snow, the majority of them motorists who had been forced to abandon their cars and seek shelter.

The host was Italian émigré Roberto Cadei, who owned the pub throughout the 1980s and remembers that night as perhaps the most chaotic in its long history. 'I just didn't know where everyone was coming from, but the only place they could come was here. The snow was so bad, you just couldn't go any further.'

With the hotel filled to capacity, a vehicle pulled into the car park with someone else seeking shelter. 'This gentleman approached me and said: "Are you in charge here?" He said to me, "Her Majesty the Queen is outside in the car," and I said, "Oh my god."'

The Queen was on her way back to Windsor Castle after visiting Princess Anne's home at Gatcombe Park, Gloucestershire. She and her entourage – two chauffeurs, two private detectives, a staff member and a lady-in-waiting – found themselves trapped in drifts about 90 m (300 ft) from the pub. The Queen had to clamber out and hurry, head down, through the storm to the hotel.

You'll thank us if this ever comes up in the royal round of a pub quiz, because the Cross Hands – an old posting house built in the fourteenth century – was about to go into the record books as the first private residence to accommodate the Queen without prior notice.

The lack of a reservation presented a couple of minor problems for Roberto. The first challenge was to get Her Majesty, Queen Elizabeth the Second, by the Grace of God Queen of this Realm and of Her other Realms and Territories, Head of the Commonwealth, Defender of the Faith, up to her room without being noticed. Luckily there was an exterior fire escape leading up to the best suite in the pub complete with bath, shower and colour television; normal price £27.80 a night for two. HM Queen settled in and Roberto headed down to serve food and attend to the rest of the travellers. But he soon received a royal command. The Queen needed to make some private phone calls – which she had to make from Roberto's flat, because the only other phone was in the public bar and it took 5 and 10 pence pieces. (Remember, the Queen never carries cash even though her face is all over it.) Then she said she rather fancied a gin and tonic.

The evening later took another surreal turn when the doorbell rang and Roberto found the racing driver Jackie Stewart and the Queen's daughter Princess Anne shivering on the step. They'd arrived to visit her mother. Roberto spent the next few hours secretly leaving the packed pub and running up and down the fire escape with trays of G & T. 'It had an air of *Fawlty Towers* to it.' A nicely apt description because Roberto's assistant manager at the time was called... Manuel.

At quarter to eleven, the roads were finally cleared and after spending seven hours at the Cross Hands the Queen left for Windsor. 'I won't forget it at all,' says Roberto. 'It will stick in my mind all my life.' The Queen didn't forget, either. She sent Roberto a Christmas card, signed by her and the Duke of Edinburgh, later that month.

OUT OF THE BOX

TV (AND RADIO) TIMES

Britain's television landscape in the early 1960s was easy to navigate. There were only two channels – BBC and ITV – and if you squinted during prime time you'd be hard pressed to tell the difference between shiny floor entertainment shows, soap operas, sitcoms and drama serials (including US imports). In terms of more cerebral programming, viewers went begging.

The Pilkington Committee was formed in 1960 to consider the future of TV. In 1962, it produced a report that largely praised the BBC's efforts in public service broadcasting, laid into ITV's reliance on imported and violent cop shows and westerns, and concluded there should be a channel that better served the loftier end of the arts and culture.

BBC Two was conceived as that highbrow retort to the rampant commercialism of ITV. It was awarded the third channel licence in 1962 ahead of its commercial rivals, in a bid to stave off more advertising on TV. But a launch night cockup meant that things got off to an inauspicious start for the channel.

BBC Two – which had been trailed by a cartoon kangaroo called Hullaballoo and her joey, Custard – was planned to launch at 7.20 p.m. on 20 April 1964. A glittering line-up included: a new sitcom, *The Alberts*; the Soviet stand-up comedian Arkady Raikin; a production of *Kiss Me, Kate*; and live fireworks from Southend Pier.

Broadcaster Denis Tuohy was the man chosen to be the face of BBC2 and launch it live on air. 'This was history,' remembers Denis, five decades on, 'and so when we'd rehearsed it so many times that the Editor said, "Let's go and have a drink", we went to the BBC bar to have a drink.'

All that rehearsing, though, would be in vain. 'I left the bar and went to the studio area and I was the only one there. So I went into the gallery and I sat there and I looked at the monitor screens and suddenly they all went dark.'

Until 6.44 p.m. on 20 April the main worry at TV Centre had been that rain would prevent the fireworks display – billed as 'Off with a bang!' in the *Radio Times*. But at 6.45 p.m. a major power cut at Battersea caused West London, and Television Centre, to black out.

BBC One moved operations to Alexandra Palace. But BBC Two was stuck in the dark. And it wasn't just the cast, crew and producers who were getting jumpy. A real kangaroo called George had been hired from London Zoo to make an appearance as the station's cartoon mascot Hullaballoo. But George panicked when the lights went out and was shunted into a scenery lift to calm him down. He then, of course, became stuck because the power cut had knocked out the elevator system.

Hearing of their new rival's plight, Associated-Rediffusion, London's commercial ITV franchise holder, kindly offered to transmit on BBC Two's behalf but the gesture was rather snootily turned down.

With five minutes to air, the execs at BBC Two asked the BBC News Centre team based at Alexandra Palace if they could launch the channel as an extra bulletin. They managed to get some pictures out, but now there was no sound. All viewers saw was newscaster Gerald Priestman mouthing apologies for the lack of service.

It was thought that no recording of that fateful night had been made at Television Centre because of the power cut, and the events became part of industry folklore... until a mysterious tape was discovered decades later in the BBC archives, based at Kingswood Warren, Surrey. The production report that came with the tape simply stated: 'Opening of BBC2'. Technician Hywel Williams was the first to realise its significance.

> The tape was made by an archivist in 1964. He or she must have been working through the night to cover the launch, recording it onto video, probably one of just a handful of recorders in the country at the time. The tape reveals that there was eventually some sound from Gerald Priestman's impromptu launch of BBC Two.

As might be expected, it lacks gravitas. Gerald Priestman says: 'Excuse me... just like Channel 1... hello? Unlike Channel 1, there's nobody there.'

By 10 p.m. that night BBC Two's technicians, who had been working by candlelight, gave up and went home. But nobody told the fireworks team at Southend. So at least something was successfully launched that night.

On 21 April 1964, BBC Two regrouped and tried again. At 11 a.m. the station was re-launched, again by presenter Dennis Tuohy who, rather sarcastically, blew out a candle as he introduced the channel's first ever programme to transmit *Play School*.

CHRISTMAS AND ALL DER TRIMMINGS

Christmas TV viewing in Britain just wouldn't be, well, Christmas without a re-run of *The Morecambe and Wise Christmas Show* from 1977. It's the one with newsreaders singing 'There is Nothin' Like a Dame' from the musical *South Pacific* and on its original transmission it drew a staggering 21 million viewers. But it's not the only British Christmas TV comedy with a place in the record books.

Every yuletide since 1962, millions of Germans gather for what has become an indisputable part of the festive celebrations. Forget singing 'Stille Nacht' around an evergreen festooned with candles. Pish to a cup of warm gloopy Eierpunsch (egg nog) and a slice of stollen! The one true mainstay of a German Christmas is a wry, 11-minute skit first written for the British stage.

It's called *Dinner For One*, and while Germans can quote from it verbatim – and often join in the punchlines – the version they watch is entirely in English. It's a New Year's Eve fixture in Germany and according to the *Guinness Book of World Records* it's the most frequently repeated TV programme *ever*, yet it's never been aired in its entirety in the UK.

Author Lauri Wylie, from Southport, wrote it for the stage, possibly as early as the 1920s, but *Dinner For One*'s first billed performance was in 1948 at the Duke of York Theatre in London. Despite its success, Wylie would die in poverty just three years later.

Dinner For One is the story of doddery aristo Miss Sophie, who throws a birthday dinner party every year. Without fail she invites her friends Sir Toby, Mr Pommeroy, Mr Winterbottom and Admiral von Schneider, but she's forgotten a small detail – they've all been dead for over a quarter of a century. Not wishing to upset her with the news, her butler, James, manfully takes up the slack by pretending to be all of the late guests – as well as playing the butler. As he serves the food and drink, he also quaffs the numerous toasts to the guests given by Miss Sophie, becoming steadily more inebriated as the evening wears on. Further challenging James is a tiger-skin rug: with the head still attached, it proves to be a health and safety nightmare. Each course begins with the signature refrain – with which the entire population of Germany chimes along:

JAMES: The same procedure as last year, madam?

SOPHIE: The same procedure as *every* year, James.

German journalist and author Philip Oltermann first saw *Dinner For One* when he was five and still hasn't tired of it.

I've seen it countless times and I can recite it by heart. Everything about it is English – the actors, the setting, and the language – there's no subtitles when it's shown. But there's something about it that has captured the German sense of humour. It's a physical slapstick sketch and the Germans love that type of comedy. It's also nostalgic and innocent.

British actor Freddie Frinton had bought the rights to the sketch and made the part of the increasingly intoxicated James his own. Frinton was famous for his stage and screen drunks but in real life was teetotal. Initially, he cast a young actress called Audrey Maye to play Sophie and the pair toured the variety theatre circuit with it. Maye left the show after a while and suggested her mother, May Warden, replace her. That lineup proved incredibly popular. The slapstick element of the show was already established, but in one performance Frinton accidentally tripped on the tiger-skin rug and the audience exploded with laughter, so he kept that in for every subsequent performance.

Freddie's widow Nora still has the rug.

He tripped over it so many hundreds and hundreds of times, it just wore out and he had to find little bits of acrylic to patch it with. He loved that sketch nearly as much as us! It was really his baby. He would be so proud if he knew how popular it would become.

In 1962, German light entertainment star Peter Frankenfeld watched Freddie pratfall his way through *Dinner For One* with May onstage in Blackpool. Frankenfeld was so charmed that he invited the pair to perform the sketch on his live TV show *GutenAbend, Peter Frankenfeld* in 1963. They were filmed live in Hamburg's Theater am Besenbinderhof, and it's that black and white recording which is so venerated. How venerated? Well, nearly 50 years on, a German newspaper,

Frankfurter Rundschau, went to the trouble of tracking down an audience member, not even shown onscreen, whose laugh is so raucous it's become an off-shoot cult all of its own. Audiences clamoured for repeats, and because the skit fits nicely as a time-filler between larger broadcasts, the German network Norddeutscher Rundfunk and its affiliates ran the snippet repeatedly in the 1960s, even reaching audiences behind the Iron Curtain in East Germany. Already much loved, *Dinner For One* was confirmed as a German tradition when it was broadcast on New Year's Eve in 1972.

In 2004, 15.6 million Germans watched *Dinner For One* and its appeal has also spread beyond Germany to Austria, Holland, Norway and even Australia.

Strangely, for a quintessentially British music hall skit, *Dinner For One* has been forgotten by the English. Says Philip Oltermann:

> I came to Britain when I was 16 and I just presumed everyone here would know *Dinner For One*, so it was a shock to realise no one I met had. I did once sit down with a VHS copy and show it to my British friends, but they weren't that impressed. I think *Dinner For One* is quite old-fashioned and in the last 50 years Britons have developed a more sophisticated comedy that's much more about wordplay than slapstick. I doubt if it was shown now that it would have anywhere near the same impact as it had in Germany.

Freddie Frinton's daughter Marilyn had to take her family to Germany to see the sketch. She said:

It was remarkable to see the audience watching my dad perform, and know it so well. If we mention Freddie over there most people have heard of him. It's amazing that so many still laugh so much, it's unbelievable actually that so many years later we're still talking about it.

WE SWEAR IT'S TRUE

When the brilliant writer and critic Kenneth Tynan dropped the F-bomb live on BBC television in 1965 – mistakenly considered by many to be the first swearword spoken on British TV – he probably had no idea that he was about to cause one of the biggest media storms of the 1960s. Tynan was nonplussed, sure that people wouldn't find the word shocking anymore. The grovelling BBC apology, the four separate House of Commons motions and the letter sent to the Queen by Mary Whitehouse urging Tynan to 'have his bottom smacked' suggested otherwise.

Given Tynan's alleged private penchant for flagellation, though, Mrs Whitehouse's admonishment might have been welcome.

The coffers of television's swear box stayed empty for a few years until newspaper columnist Peregrine Worsthorne came over all pottymouthed in 1973. When asked to comment on live TV about how the public would react to a cabinet minister's recently exposed affair Worsthone suggested, in no uncertain terms, that the public 'wouldn't give a f***'. Concisely put, but it cost him dear. He had been slated to become editor of the *Daily Telegraph* and the offer was now quickly withdrawn.

In 1976 the Sex Pistols, egged on by presenter Bill Grundy, scandalised television watchers throughout the land with a string of swear words that prompted a TV ban for the band, a *Sun* headline 'The Filth and The Fury', and a general media and establishment fatwa on Punk – which, of course, was the making of it. The clip seems rather tame now. What's most interesting to modern eyes watching it (and ears listening) is not the profanities but the use of the wonderfully archaic term 'rotter' as spat by Pistol's guitarist Steve Jones. Why 'rotter' didn't re-enter youth parlance is a mystery – it should have, it's a brilliant word.

In 2004 former Pistol John Lydon (aka Rotten) was a contestant on *I'm A Celebrity... Get Me Out Of Here!* Towards the end of one episode he was clearly heard to call the audience 'f***ing c***s' after learning that he had not been voted off. His outburst generated less than 100 complaints to TV regulators Ofcom. What a rotter.

SHOUT OUT TO MY X-FILES

Broadcasting from another era, the mysterious and very creepy 'numbers stations' can still be chanced upon if you've got some patience – and a shortwave analogue radio. Numbers stations are like no radio show you'll have heard before. Dating from the Cold War, they transmit on hidden frequencies, their playlists and shoutouts consisting of strings of cryptic numbers recited in strange voices, or high-pitch bleeps of code. Many think, but few officially state, that these are designed for spies 'in the field' to pick up.

At the apex of the Cold War, radio lovers across the globe started to notice bizarre broadcasts on the airwaves. Starting with a weird melody or the sound of several beeps, these transmissions might be followed by the unnerving sound of a strange woman's voice counting in German or the voice of a child reciting letters in English.

Initially baffled, ham radio enthusiasts at the time eventually realised that these sounds were in fact secret codes, enabling government agencies to transmit messages to spies from across the globe. Specific broadcasts soon gained loyal followers who'd tune in every night and who gave them colourful names like Nancy Adam Susan, The Lincolnshire Poacher, The Swedish Rhapsody or The Gong Station.

Times have changed and technology has evolved, but there's evidence that this old-fashioned method of communication might still be used. Shortwave numbers stations might seem low-tech, but when computers can now so easily be hacked they might remain the best option for transmitting information.

Akin Fernandez is the creator of the Conet Project, a comprehensive archive of the phenomenon of numbers stations. He explains why the system is so flawless. 'It's completely secure because the messages can't be tracked, the recipient could be anywhere. You just send the spies to a country and get them to buy a radio. They know where to tune and when.'

Some have claimed that the numbers are an elaborate prank, or an urban myth, but the sheer number of them, and the longevity of some of the broadcasts, is equally compelling for believers. In spite of all the clues, no government has ever officially admitted or denied using numbers stations, nor have intelligence agencies. Well they wouldn't, would they?

ATTENBOROUGH'S BIG BREAK

Launched in 1954, *Zoo Quest* established the BBC as a world leader in natural history television. But it was an unfortunate twist of fate that would turn its producer David Attenborough into the most famous onscreen face in British TV history.

Zoo Quest was television's first regularly scheduled natural history series, and arguably the father of the entire genre. It followed zoologists from London Zoo on adventures to remote locations in order to collect animal species. The show was groundbreaking, bringing exotic locations and species into the living rooms of ordinary Britons.

Jack Lester, then the curator of *London Zoo*'s reptile house, suggested the show when he invited his friend David Attenborough to bring a film crew along on a snake-hunting mission to Sierra Leone. The idea was that Attenborough would produce the films on location and, back in Britain, Lester would top and tail that report with an in-studio chat. The animal brought back from the trip would also feature live in the studio.

The standard 35 mm cameras would have been too bulky and costly to bring along, and the pitch was rejected by the BBC until Attenborough convinced them that just as good results could be achieved on smaller 16 mm cameras and a budget of £900.

The series was a ratings magnet from the first episode. Tragically, however, Lester caught an unknown tropical disease and died two years later. Attenborough was left to handle the studio introductions as well. Despite his reluctance, he quickly became the BBC's face of natural history, a position that was cemented by the broadcast of *Zoo Quest for a Dragon* (1956), in which the team went in search of the Komodo dragon. Footage of the Komodo was a television landmark, but problems with an export permit meant the dragon stayed put.

There then came a shift of opinion among natural history experts, who began to argue against the capture of wild animals and their transfer to captivity. Attenborough agreed and called time on *Zoo Quest*.

(If any readers have information as to what Mr Attenborough has been up to since, please contact the publishers.)

CLOUDY VISION

On November 1936, the BBC unfurled the world's first television weather chart over which a disembodied voice tried to explain what was going on with all the arrows and swirly lines. Two years later, the chart was rolled up when television ceased broadcasting for the duration of the Second World War. Once hostilities were over the weather map was pressed into service again, lasting until 1954 when efforts were made to simplify and humanise the reports. On 11 January 1954, George Cowling of the Met Office became the first person to present a live weather forecast on British television. The *Radio Times* for that week highlighted the new service, reassuring readers that Cowling was not only qualified for the job but was married and had children. The budget for the weather forecast was £50, which included the easel displaying the map.

It was the Met Office that began to provide weather reports for the BBC in 1923. It continued to do so for 96 years, and then in 2016 the broadcaster awarded the contract to Met Office rivals MeteoGroup.

NOT A CROSS WORD ABOUT *CROSSROADS*

Wobbly sets, overwrought plot lines about washing up, forgetful actors, a steadfast refusal to just go away – and one of the greatest TV theme tunes ever. It could only be *Crossroads*.

The West Midlands' answer to *Coronation Street*, *Crossroads* was set in the glittering, occasionally cut-throat and unintentionally surreal world of a medium-sized motel with convenient access to the freshly laid M1 motorway.

When it launched in 1964, there were high hopes for a shiny new breed of soap that would wash away the grit and tar of the provinces, as trademarked by *Coronation Street* just a few miles up the road in Salford. The very idea of the show, commissioned by Lew Grade, was fresh. The idea of a motel – an American word, modern, aspirational, sexy – oozed sophistication and, taking another cue from across the pond, the show was deliberately formatted to run five times a week. The cherry on top of this glamorous soap cake was Tony Hatch's fabulous theme tune, which twanged splendidly as the credits crisscrossed the screen.

The critics hated the show from the start. Yet it struck a chord with the public and trounced rival daytime soaps like *General Hospital*. It was made on a shoestring budget and the sheer volume of episodes meant that scripts had to be churned out, so much of the inspiration came from that day's papers. The storylines captured a Britain that was rapidly changing. At the helm was a strong female businesswoman Meg Richardson (later Mortimer) played by Noele Gordon. Disabled, ethnic minority and even openly gay characters had meaningful roles and storylines covered drug abuse, gambling addiction, mental health, divorce, rape, terrorism, racism and, er, Satanic witchcraft – none of which had ever been tackled in a British soap, let alone in daytime.

It was originally planned to have a six-week run and be shown in just three regions, but by the 1970s *Crossroads* was sometimes peaking at 15 million viewers in spite of its after-noon slot. Those are the sort of audience figures *Coronation Street* was getting in prime time.

Part of *Crossroads*' quirky charm was, of course, its flaws. The cheap sets really did wobble, actors fluffed their lines and characters just disappeared. Benny, the woolly hat-wearing village idiot was last seen on screen ascending a ladder to put a fairy on the Christmas Tree – as far as anyone knows, he's still at the top of that ladder.

Many agree that the show really lost the plot in 1981, with the sacking of Noele Gordon. Viewers were genuinely outraged at the decision and ATV execs received threatening calls and excrement sent through the post. Noele wasn't chuffed about it either. Her character waved goodbye from a cabin on the *QE2*, and, like Banquo's ghost turned up to that year's ATV Christmas party to perform a specially written and terrifically mean-spirited song for the head of the channel. It was, all agreed (and there's film online to prove it), both excruciating and yet very *Crossroads*.

After Noele left, *Crossroads* began to haemorrhage viewers. In spite of a relaunch by the Central ITV franchise after ATV lost its licence, it floundered against a tide of imported Aussie soaps. The show sank in 1988 but in 2000 was relaunched, not once but twice. The first attempt added storylines from the nearby village, the second tried too hard to be ironic, with knowingly camp scripts that only sucked dry what little charm the show had left.

AND FINALLY

In the 1980s British squaddies stationed in the Falkland Islands were banned from calling the islanders 'Bennies', in reference to the *Crossroad*'s character; their seniors considered it derogatory. After that they referred to them as 'Stills', as in 'Still Bennies'.

SECRETS AND LIES

DID THE EAGLE LAND?

In the summer of 1940, Britain suffered its biggest military defeat of the Second World War. The advancing German Army pushed British forces out of France, and nearly a quarter of a million troops fled from Dunkirk. Fear of a Nazi invasion loomed large on the horizon.

No one felt the threat more than those living along the Suffolk coast in East Anglia. There had been fortifications on these shores since the eighteenth century, when the country feared invasion by Napoleon. In the Second World War, the threat from Nazi Germany was no less real. So real in fact, that many believe an invasion actually happened – despite the government officially maintaining that no German invaders ever set foot on British soil.

From the outset of the war an entire stretch of this coastline – including the village of Shingle Street – was evacuated for top secret military use. It was closed entirely to the public and rumours abounded, many people assuming that it was used for experimental weapons development. Partial release of secret documents in 1993 revealed that an uncharged chemical bomb was tested in the local pub of Shingle Street. But some soldiers and civilians working in the area believed that something far more shocking happened.

One night in August 1940, witnesses claimed to have seen Germans landing on the beach. The invasion was repelled in a particularly gruesome fashion; as the enemy leapt from their landing craft, they were burnt alive in a wall of flames that came from beneath the sea. The beach, some have testified, was littered with the charred remains of German soldiers.

In 1940 Sonny Ambrose was a 2nd Lieutenant with the Royal Engineers. Sonny's relatives, Sue and Margaret, recollect the event that changed his life forever. 'According to Sonny, when the tide was low they put pipes out on the sand or in the sand and filled them with petrol,' says Sue. Sonny claimed he was told the Germans were coming and that he would have to set fire to the water. Sue continues, '... it gave him nightmares all the time, as he could hear the screaming and yelling of those who were getting burnt alive.' Margaret tells of the difference in Sonny's personality after the event, 'He was so full of life, enjoyed life so much... he changed completely.'

All the witnesses are now dead, but testimony remains from many of them. In 1992 in the local *Evening Star*, Rose Aldous tells of her husband collecting corpses from Shingle Street. 'He said he had picked up dead bodies – Germans.' In the *East Anglia Daily Times*, John Rux Burton describes how 'The beach was covered in dozens of charred bodies... My grandfather was devastated by it all.' There are at least six other accounts telling the same story; it's enough to make you wonder. But what's the truth? Did Germans really land at Shingle Street? Did the sea really catch fire?

The loss of soldiers, weaponry and equipment at Dunkirk meant other methods of defence were needed. Historian James Hayward, an expert on the defence of the east coast of Britain during the war, goes into more detail. 'In the summer of 1940 the petroleum warfare department was formed with the idea of using petroleum offensively against the enemy. One of the ideas they came up with was using it as a "sea flame barrage".'

However far-fetched it seems – and it does sound like something H.G. Wells might have come up with – old newsreel footage shows us that the technology in question did exist at the time. The voiceover paints a wonderful sci-fi picture (in the best received pronunciation): 'From submarine pipelines oil bubbles to the surface. As the dark patches merge together, they're electrically ignited from the shore and the sea bursts into flame.'

But James Hayward doesn't believe they were ever used on Shingle Street. 'There's no evidence of charred bodies being washed up here, and there never was a flame barrage anywhere in this location.' He goes on to say that a couple of German airmen were washed up on the beach and that might have been part of the confusion. But why does he think these stories started? 'There was a great propaganda campaign to spread this story of flame barrages and invasions that had failed because we needed to convince America that we were still in the game, we were going to fight back against Hitler.'

Whatever the true story might be, the Ministry of Defence continues to deny that the invasion of Shingle Street ever took place. But for some local people it will be forever etched in their family history as the day the Nazis were defeated and the sea caught fire.

STARLITE

On 22 August 1985, the runway of Manchester Airport saw one of the worst aircraft disasters in British history. A Boeing 737, operating as British Airtours Flight 28M and about to depart for Corfu with 131 passengers, caught fire before it had even taken off. Fifty-three passengers and two crew members died in just 40 seconds that day, but only seven as a result of burns. Most of the deaths were caused by toxic fumes from the burning plastics inside the aircraft.

The disaster played on the mind of a Hartlepool hairdresser, Maurice Ward. In his spare time he experimented with the production of new hair products – shampoo, conditioners, dyes and perms. Maurice was a man with a curious mind, whose concoctions made him something of a celebrity in local hairdressing circles. By the time of the airport fire he had shut up shop to indulge in his passion for chemistry.

Could this amateur chemist come up with a plastic that could withstand extreme temperatures and not give off lethal gases? He began making up teaspoonfuls of what he described as 'stuff' in a food mixer at his home, blending up to 20 different formulations a day. Eventually, he created a few plastic blends that he liked and subsequently bought a machine which could help turn those lumps of plastic into sheets. He began rolling out his samples of 'stuff' and tested them with a blow-torch. The material appeared to resist temperatures of 2,500°C (4,532°F), yet stay cool enough to touch. Considering 'stuff' to be a rather ordinary description for such an extraordinary substance, he renamed it 'Starlite'.

It seemed that Ward, the amateur inventor, had created something which the world of science had tried and failed to achieve for years. The possibilities for this wonder material were limitless – if only he could be taken seriously. But whether rivals thought he was a joke or were developing their own product, Britain's chemical companies sent him packing.

Someone who did take Maurice seriously was a researcher for the BBC's primetime science show, *Tomorrow's World*. Recorded live for the show, a chicken's egg was coated with Starlite and then subjected to the full force of a blowtorch. No one in the studio or watching at home at the BBC on 8 March 1990 could believe what they were seeing. Peter McCann was the presenter who put Starlite through its paces. It remains one of the show's most memorable demonstrations, and a transcript from the transmission captures Peter's incredulity.

Well… it hasn't broken up at all, you can see on the front here it is glowing red-hot. But just watch this: if I turn the flame off (and remember that it was producing 1,200 degrees of heat), and I take that charred bit, and I put it flat in the palm of my hand… and it only just feels warm? And then if I then crack it open, what's more, the egg… hasn't even begun to start cooking.

Today McCann remembers that moment as one of the most incredible experiments he ever did on *Tomorrow's World*.

The egg's extraordinary resistance to the blowtorch's heat came from the thin layer of Starlite that Maurice had carefully painted onto its shell before the show. Put it this way, if you train a blowtorch onto an untreated egg it explodes in an instant.

We knew very little about Starlite. I remember asking Maurice about it after the show. He came across as a very secretive man, who stayed behind the cameras, but he didn't let Starlite out of his sight. He said it was too precious for him to talk about.

I remember it was white and like a type of plastic, almost feeling like rubber to the touch. After I turned the blowtorch off during the show I was really nervous about picking the egg up… we'd not been given another egg to rehearse on, and I wasn't at all sure it wouldn't burn my hand, but it was hardly warm. Incredible.

Ironically for a substance invented to keep things cool, Maurice's creation had the reverse effect on the show's hotline, sending it into meltdown. 'Normally we'd have five or six people contacting the show after we showed a good new invention. But this was incredible,' enthuses McCann. 'We had thousands of people wanting to know more about Starlite.'

Could it now realise its commercial potential? After its debut on *Tomorrow's World*, Ward was hailed as the man with the Billionaire Brain. Scientists, multinational companies and even NASA were soon rushing to get their hands on Starlite. There was talk of million-dollar deals. But then… nothing.

Why?

Ward wasn't just a clever man he was also cautious, overly

so. It took 18 months before he allowed the Ministry of Defence to take a closer look at Starlite. Sir Ronald Mason was one of their top scientific advisors and the man they sent to delve a little deeper. 'Scientists had been trying to get something to withstand a nuclear flash for years, and Starlite appeared to outperform anything seen before,' he says. At first it wasn't clear how the substance worked; was it diffusing, absorbing or reflecting heat? Sir Ronald explains his findings:

> It transpired that it was a 'smart material'. A substance that responds and reacts to an event. We could have used it in a variety of ways – from the protection of structures in naval vessels and aircraft interiors to making safe electrical cables – anything that needed protecting from heat and burning. Devastating fires could be made a thing of the past, both in the home and in industry, with significant benefit in saving lives.

Though Ward's secretiveness remained a frustration, the fact that someone like Maurice could stumble upon such a ground-breaking material impressed Sir Ronald.

> There's a hell of a lot of complex chemistry that goes into perming and shampooing hair... making it up and dyeing and so on, the surface chemistry of dyes being absorbed onto hair and repairing hair. I have a feeling that Maurice recognised the similarity between some of the things he was playing with in the hair dressing salon and some of the materials that turn up in the books on fire retardants, for example. Intuition, as you know, always has a lot to do with scientific discovery and invention in any sphere of life.

Starlite was like nothing the Ministry of Defence had ever seen before: it withstood simulated nuclear blasts and high-powered lasers during the testing process. The fact that each batch was slightly different meant that they weren't able to help Maurice optimise its performance. Ever suspicious, he wouldn't let the material out of his sight, a slight problem for those trying to harness its commercial potential. Sir Ronald believes the chemicals used in the formulas were those he had at his hair salon, which might explain his reluctance to share. As Sir Ronald says, 'I think that actually the ingredients of Starlite were easily obtainable and easily made up, and he didn't want anyone to discover how easy it was to make.'

He did once let a sample out of his sight, but only under SAS guard to be sent to NASA for nuclear testing. That too was a triumph; Starlite was found to be able to withstand the force of 75 Hiroshima bombs.

Maurice truly believed his invention was worth billions, but he continued to refuse all requests to provide samples for testing that might enable a company to analyze the substance and discover its composition. Ward's story is at turns as inspirational as it is infuriating, a genuine case of a backyard boffin making a world-changing discovery but never allowing it to realise its potential.

Maurice died in 2011 and Starlite burnt out with him. He left behind no known pieces of it nor a known recipe. But he did leave a tantalising clue. When one journalist asked him what was in it, he simply replied, 'Oh, just a bit of flour and baking powder.'

THE TOP SECRET BAKERY FULL OF THE WRONG KIND OF DOUGH

During the Second World War, when Britain's food factories were the target of German bombs and food was rationed, the people of Bristol welcomed news that a new bakery was to be built by the Co-operative Society under the auspices of their building manager Edward W. Bracey. But that eager anticipation of fresh baked buns, loaves and pastries was replaced by suspicion and disappointment because there was a marked lack of the scent of warm yeasty dough in the air.

The locals didn't know it at the time, but the bakery was a front and the Co-op was, er, cooperating with the US government.

It started with a furtive telephone call to Bracey and a request that he meet a US Army officer at Bristol Temple Meads railway station. From there Bracey would be escorted to the War Office in London. It was here that the man from the Co-op met none other than the Supreme Allied Commander of the Allied Expeditionary Force, General Dwight Eisenhower. Dwight's message: 'Build that bakery at once.'

But why did the ovens stay cold?

The Bristol Records Office holds the original plans for the bakery and in them there's nothing to show the secret purpose to which the bakery was going to be put, although one letter attached to the drawings does reveal Edward Bracey's almost obsessive interest in the drainage system beneath the building. In fact, Bracey was building bombproof shelters in the bakery, which would be protected by armed guards.

Local historian and journalist Eugene Byrne elaborates: 'What's in that bakery gives away all the invasion plans for D-Day. The bakery was a top secret storage facility for French currency and American military maps.' Had German spies discovered that 20 million French Francs were being stored by the Americans, they could be sure that the invasion would take place in France. Byrne continues, 'But what's even more important is that the maps, which were being stored for issue to American soldiers and more particularly to American officers, were very detailed and up to date showing the areas in which they were going to be fighting, and those maps were of Normandy.'

The people of Bristol were used to seeing GIs all over the city, on duty in barracks and on weekend passes in the pubs and dance halls, but suddenly there was an unusually large number of Americans milling around that silent bakery. Those civilians that noticed may have heeded that loose lips sink ships and passed unquestioning. But for some citizens – especially if they were of a certain age – it meant one thing only: more sweets.

Vic Williams was an 11-year-old boy at the time and remembers well the Americans around the factory. 'I must have heard about it from other children at school. They said the bakery in Whitby Road was a good place to get chewing gum. The officers seemed to have more sweets than the privates and I don't recall seeing many privates there.'

As all children should, Williams saw the presence of these officers, plus their Jeeps, as a source of entertainment and free treats rather than a cause for suspicion, but did he know what was going on? 'Well, I know we can remember going there quite a few times and all of a sudden they disappeared.'

On 6 June 1944 the Jeeps, maps and the money were all headed to France and on the very same day the bakery was handed back to Edward Bracey. He received this letter of thanks from a senior officer in the US Army:

Dear Sir,

I want to express my sincere appreciation of the splendid cooperation and advice which we received from you during the period of reconstruction of the Brislington Bakery. It is my hope that your substantial contribution to the war effort will prove as great a source of satisfaction to you as it has been helpful to us.

Having kept up his part in this strictly knead-to-dough, sorry, need-to-know secret, Bracey was given the go-ahead to complete the works at the bakery – which opened for legitimate business within weeks of D-Day.

MACHINE GUN MYSTERY

In the early 1880s, William Cantelo announced to his family that he'd perfected a new invention, a rapid firing automatic gun, which he believed would revolutionise warfare. Then the Victorian engineer packed his bags and was never seen again.

Could he have travelled to the United States and assumed a new identity?

Shortly after Cantelo's disappearance, an American called Hiram Maxim patented his own automatic weapon, and it's Maxim who is now credited as the inventor of the machine gun. But the modern branch of the Cantelo family believe that their ancestor and Hiram Maxim might just be one and the same.

William Cantelo was a pub landlord from Southampton

with a private passion for inventing things. He kept the details of his work a closely guarded secret by working in the underground tunnels beneath his establishment, but neighbours at the time often reported hearing sounds not unlike rapid gunfire coming from below the streets. Once Cantelo disappeared, the tunnels fell silent. His closest family knew he was developing a special gun, but when Hiram Maxim's automatic machine gun was made public... it was exactly the same.

Looking at the leap forward in the weapon design of the 1880s, Jonathan Ferguson, the Curator of Firearms at Fort Nelson, says that the key to Maxim's design 'was to exploit the energy stored in the cartridge; not just to push the bullet out of the barrel but to drive the working parts of the gun back and then forwards again, picking up another round, pushing into the chamber and then firing it for as long as you hold down the trigger.'

Though the physics behind these weapons of mass destruction is fascinating, what's really interesting is whether or not there's a chance that Maxim and Cantelo could have invented the same kind of gun at exactly the same time? 'It's possible that more than one inventor was working on new forms of rapid fire gun,' says Ferguson. 'You start the century with flintlock muskets and end it with machine guns. So you can't rule out the idea that more than one guy was working on something along these lines.'

The mystery behind Cantelo's disappearance has perplexed his family for more than 130 years, especially with the discovery that a large sum of money was transferred out of his bank account and nobody knows where it went. Perhaps Cantelo was paying the way for a new life.

Years after Cantelo went missing, a series of run-ins with Maxim led the family to believe that he was indeed the same person. Maxim was born in America, but he moved to Britain at the age of 41. Shortly after he arrived in London, Cantelo's sons saw a picture of him in the newspaper. Due to the similarities with their father they were convinced it was him. After a line of enquiry taking them, literally, round the houses, they managed to track him down to Waterloo station just as he was boarding a train.

The story has become part of the family's history and Barry Cantelo, the great-great-grandson of William, has spent more than 40 years researching his curious ancestor. Of the near miss at Waterloo, Barry says:

> The boys saw the man that they addressed as father… they pleaded with him, 'Come home and see mother.' Sadly, it was the point of departure for the train. The man turned to them and said, 'Hello, boys,' but the train was leaving. So he hopped on board and away he went… the only difference being that he had a slight American accent.'

This incident quite rightly disturbed the boys, who returned home to their mother convinced that the man in question was their father.

Though it seems unlikely that the sons would report seeing their father if they weren't certain, it's perhaps best to leave the final say to science, lest we be swayed by sentiment. Professor Mark Nixon is a pioneer in face recognition technology, who has compared the family's only illustration of William Cantelo with a photograph of Hiram Maxim, taken at a later stage in his life but similarly bearded. Their ages may be different, but could they be the same person?

Nixon acknowledges the similarities between the pair and notes: 'You see that the hairline might be in the same place. The nose appears to be in a similar place, the mouth appears to be in a similar place.' So far so good, but the pose is not the same in the two photographs, which creates ambiguity, 'There appears to be some differences too… And there's a lot of stuff we can't see. We cannot exactly see the ear that could be a clincher.'

So yet one more dead end in the family mystery. The baffling circumstances surrounding Cantelo's disappearance have never been fully explained. Maxim writes in his autobiography that a man was impersonating him in the USA whilst he was in Britain. Was it a case of mistaken identity? Or was Maxim just putting people off the scent?

STRANGE DAYS

HERE'S THE NEWS: IT'S THE END OF THE WORLD, WE'RE ALL DOOMED. AND COMING UP... *THE SOUND OF MUSIC*

If the nuclear balloon went up – and until the end of the Cold War in the 1990s that *was* a distinct possibility – surviving British citizens might have noticed a few changes to their day-to-day routine. But thanks to the cheerful-sounding Wartime Broadcasting Service (WBS) there would, at least, be some continuity from the airwaves – for two hours a day, until your batteries ran out...

The WBS was an emergency BBC radio station based in a network of bunkers at Wood Norton; a Grade II listed Victorian stately home near Evesham in Worcestershire. Here, using prerecorded and live broadcasts, the BBC made preparations to keep the nation not just informed but also entertained.

Situated some miles away from any anticipated targets, Wood Norton's bunkers were specially adapted to withstand first the firestorms and then the long weeks of precipitation of radioactive fallout. Around 90 BBC staff – from engineers to news gatherers – would have been stationed here. Originally they would have been designated to Wood Norton whether they wanted to work the end of the world shift or not. Later, staff with the right credentials were given the choice – and some did opt out, preferring to die, or at least take their chances with their families.

The emergency broadcasts would be transmitted via the radio masts at Droitwich, which were, and still are, powerful enough to beam Wood Norton's output across the UK, picked up and relayed on by the BBC's regional teams.

'It was all run on behalf of the government by the BBC,' says Michael Hodder, former head of the Wartime Broadcasting Service, 'scheduled to start if there had been a time of tension leading to a nuclear exchange.' Recently released under the Freedom of Information Act, this is a transcript of the chilling opening message:

'This is the Wartime Broadcasting Service. This country has been attacked with nuclear weapons… stay tuned to this wavelength, stay calm and stay in your own homes.'

Michael Hodder still shivers to think about the broadcasts. 'This felt very real to me because I had gone through the 1962 Cuban Missile Crisis and I can remember going to bed that evening in 1962 and wondering whether I'd be alive the next morning.' Between the gloomy bulletins advising folk to stay in their homes there was, at least, a schedule of pleasantly distracting programmes.

We had a locker full of light entertainment, recorded on cassette, like *Hancock's Half Hour*, *Round the Horne* and *Just a Minute*. We also had *The Sound of Music* [the soundtrack album from the 1965 smash hit film]. If there had been a nuclear attack, people would still have heard the BBC and hopefully they would have taken heart and said to one another, 'The BBC is still broadcasting, therefore hopefully we're going to be alright.'

So, the plans were all in place to ensure that the end of the world wouldn't be filled with any, ahem, dead air. Who would be the presenter? That couldn't be agreed upon – and, thanks to the Official Secrets Act, we might never know.

But we have some clues as to who might have been in the frame. Released secret memos from 1974 tell us that senior civil servants insisted only a recognisable broadcaster should be used because an unfamiliar voice might give the impression that Auntie had been 'obliterated'.

Newscasters Angela Rippon and Richard Baker, chat show host Michael Parkinson and current affairs presenter Frank Bough were all considered, but none had the requisite security clearance. The avuncular Bough was, in the 1970s, the presenter of *Nationwide*, the early evening magazine show that was very much the grand-daddy of *The One Show*. It would have been the equivalent of *The One Show*'s Matt Baker telling us to stay in our homes as the UK ceases to exist and then linking to a prerecorded tape about Dartmoor ponies getting a haircut. The only person who did tick the right security boxes was a recently retired and relatively unknown newsreader called Hugh Searight.

The WBS came under fire from some quarters, who said the whole plan was hogwash, a public calming measure that couldn't be guaranteed to work since no one even knew if the radio waves would get through against the radioactive fallout.

Nonetheless, there was a specialist team at the transmitter on permanent standby to flick the requisite switches and dials.

John Phillips was a radio engineer at Droitwich from 1943 to 1986. 'As far as we were concerned, we would have to transmit the wartime emergency programme whatever was happening. That was part of the job and we had to go through the motions. Whether anybody was there to listen to us or not, we wouldn't know.'

That heart-in-the-throat realisation that the WBS was going live would have been preceded by a telephone call to John from a civil servant known only by a codename – Ringmaster. There had been plenty of exercises as well as close-to-the-edge moments (especially following the Soviet invasion of Afghanistan in 1979), so John knew the drill intimately. 'Ringmaster would tell us to follow a certain procedure, which was laid down in a publication called the *War Book*. As far as I can remember we never got as far as a message saying, "Man the shelters", but it was all very clandestine.' John says that had the worst happened, he hoped the entertainment schedule would have included episodes of *The Goon Show*. 'At least I would have died laughing.'

Sadly, had the apocalypse arrived after 1993, we would have all been dying for a laugh because the BBC dropped the Light Entertainment shows. The reasoning was that listeners would drain their precious batteries attempting to cling on to normality by chuckling along to old sitcoms as they pulled clumps of irradiated hair from their heads. Only official announcements would be broadcast at set times so that survivors could keep radio usage to a minimum.

The late BBC newsreader Peter Donaldson was the voice of

the last, and, who knows, present, prerecorded announcement of war:

> 'This is the Wartime Broadcasting Service. This country has been attacked with nuclear weapons. Communications have been severely disrupted, and the number of casualties and the extent of the damage are not yet known. We shall bring you further information as soon as possible. Meanwhile, stay tuned to this wavelength, stay calm and stay in your own homes.'

Michael Hodder says that after this was recorded he and Peter shared a bottle of whisky – and who could blame them? Peter died in 2015 and the recording, in its entirety, was played at his funeral.

'The last time the WBS readied itself to head to the bunkers was as recent as 1989,' says Michael Hodder. 'There was widespread jubilation as the Berlin wall fell, but behind the scenes there were genuine concerns that the Soviet Union could have retaliated.'

Luckily we never did get to hear the wartime schedule. So far, anyway. A Wartime Broadcasting Service, probably, still exists and there are still, probably, engineers like John Phillips, ready to hit a button and turn a dial to an emergency wavelength. Better stock up on batteries.

HERE'S THE NEWS. THERE ISN'T ANY

A nuclear day of reckoning is likely to be a strange one in any broadcaster's book, but really as strange as having nothing to report at all? In 1930, with broadcasting still in its infancy, listening to the evening news was a family event that was treated with real deference. Imagine, then, the collective disappointment of three million licence holders (according to BBC official figures for 1930) on 18 April, when the plummy newscaster, without a trace of irony, announced: 'Good evening. Today is Good Friday. There is no news,' and put a record of piano music on instead. Such an event happening today is unimaginable; even in 1930 the idea was ridiculous. But there was more than met the ear on 'No News Day'. The BBC was simply following the accepted code of the time.

What exactly does that mean? Well, just four years earlier, Lord Reith, the Director-General of the BBC, had announced the end of the 1926 General Strike and then handed over the microphone to the Prime Minister. Today a PM broadcasting the news would not be viewed as impartial reporting, but it was an age of deference and there was a general agreement regarding what the public should hear about.

Now, on Friday April 18 1930, the Home Secretary gave an interview to a newspaper, which the Home Office subsequently wanted to deny. Since it was the Easter Bank Holiday weekend there would be no newspapers printed, and, the thinking was, if there was no other media comment then the story would be dead by Tuesday. The BBC agreed not to report. In fact, they didn't bother reporting anything at all. Today there is so much news and comment sloshing through the airwaves that we are finding it increasingly difficult to distinguish what 'news' actually is and whether there's enough of it to fulfil the insatiable modern demand for it. Just ask BBC royal correspondent Nicholas Witchell. When asked for yet another update on progress following the hours and hours of live broadcasting around the birth of Prince George, he told the studio, 'The news is… there's no news.'

AN UNHAPPY MEDIUM

Helen Duncan was not the last person in Britain to be tried under the Witchcraft Act of 1753, but it was her case that was the most celebrated in modern times and it directly led to the Act's repeal, on 22 June 1951.

Helen wasn't a witch, per se. She billed herself and operated as a spiritualist-medium – in fact, a rather poor one, since she'd been exposed as a fake on a number of occasions. But in late November 1941, at a public séance in Portsmouth, she contacted the ghost of a sailor killed in action on HMS *Barham*. News of this spread like wildfire across the maritime city and Helen found herself inundated with requests from families with relatives on the ship.

What was most extraordinary about the story was that HMS *Barham* had indeed been sunk on 21 November 1941, but her loss had not yet been announced. On patrol in the central Mediterranean, *Barham* was struck by three of four torpedoes fired by German submarine *U-331* and the ship's magazine exploded. Of its crew, 862 were killed. The disaster was immediately made a state secret to spare the morale back home and keep the Germans in the dark. (Germany knew the ship had gone down, the U-boat captain was awarded an Iron Cross the same day, but they presumably didn't know the number of casualties.) The Admiralty didn't officially announce *Barham*'s loss until January the following year.

The Royal Navy traced the rumours about HMS *Barham* to Helen's séance and began to plant their own spooks in her meetings. Ruling out a hotline to the other side, they wondered how she got the information. It then transpired that before the Admiralty tried to suppress the story *The Times* had managed to report it in brief after the news was mistakenly leaked – so Helen might have read that.

Either way, with Helen's ability to attract a crowd now greater than ever and mass mobilisations underway for the still top secret D-Day invasions, nobody could afford any fluke predictions. While she was midway through another séance in 1944, the police swooped. They arrested Helen using the only law they could draw on: the Witchcraft Act.

The first Witchcraft Act came into law in 1542 – a period in British history when there was such a fear of actual witchcraft that legislation was needed to provide a means of standardising the punishment of it, usually death. What happened, of course, was that the Act simply became a justification for mutilating and killing people, usually women – for the most spurious reasons and at the drop of a (pointy) hat.

Over the centuries, it was replaced with subsequent Witchcrafts Act, some more merciful than others. The Act of 1735 was almost solely intended to legislate against those charlatans and fortune-tellers who made money preying on the vulnerable and recently bereaved, and against those who even claimed to be witches. Even more generally, just making stuff up about ghosts was frowned upon – so there was plenty to cover the security services if Helen's arrest looked dodgy. Helen had always been horrified at being called a witch, so being charged under the Witchcraft Act was a bitter pill for her to swallow. A trial by jury was set for the Old Bailey and a media frenzy ensued. Helen was given the soubriquet Hellish Nell.

Helen was sentenced to ten weeks in Holloway and banned from holding séances. Ten years later, in November 1956, she was arrested again, this time under the Fraudulent Mediums Act 1951 – the very statute inspired by her case – but she was released with a caution.

A released memo from the period of the trial at the Old Bailey revealed how furious Winston Churchill was with the Admiralty for pursuing the case in the first place.

> Let me have a report on why the Witchcraft Act 1735 was used in a modern court of justice. What was the cost of this trial to the State, observing that witnesses were brought from Portsmouth and maintained here in this crowded London for a fortnight, and the Recorder kept busy with all this absolute tomfoolery, to the detriment of necessary work in the Courts.

Helen died on 6 December 1956, shortly after her final run-in with the law, but her family have continued to campaign for her name to be cleared of practising witchcraft. She was, they say, a gifted medium, nothing more.

THOMAS DUFFY'S UNLUCKY NUMBER

On 7 July 1937, newspapers announced the first arrest as a result of a call to the newly launched emergency number, 999. Mrs Stanley Beard frantically dialled her way into history as her husband grappled with a burglar called Thomas Duffy in the parlour of their semi in Hampstead, London.

Before the emergency services had a dedicated number, the public could only dial 0 and then wait in a queue for an operator to connect them. Since police and fire stations rarely had more than a single telephone, callers would often then be greeted by an engaged tone. It was this convoluted system that had contributed to the deaths of five women in a house fire in Marylebone when the fire brigade couldn't be contacted.

In 1935, the General Post Office was tasked by the government to find a solution. They suggested a switchboard where operators gave priority to emergency calls; these would be announced by a large klaxon horn in the call centres – and they were up until the 1960s. For civilians, an easy-to-remember, three-digit number was proposed. The number 9, one hole away from the dial stop, was the easiest number to find on a phone in the dark, and rotating the dial to the full extent three times summoned help.

When it launched in 1937, the service was available in only a few square miles of London. Private telephones in houses were still rare in Britain, and converting the nation's telephone boxes to accept free emergency calls was a mammoth task that would take time to complete.

Unluckily for burglar Thomas, he chose to break into one of the few homes in Britain that had a private telephone and which was was in the 999 catchment. At 4.20 a.m. on 2 July,

Mr Stanley Beard caught Duffy red-handed and Mrs Stanley Beard called the police at Scotland Yard, thus proving the GPO's theory about the memorability of the triple 9. The police arrested the burglar within five minutes of the call being made. Later, Mr Beard told the magistrates' court that he was very impressed by the new system and that it was probably one of only a handful of things worth paying taxes for.

Generally the dedicated emergency number was a great success. During the launch week 1,336 calls had been made on the special number: 1,073 were genuine, 171 were prank calls and 92 were calls by the public checking to see if the 999 system was working. The Met's response was to issue a wry, but deadly serious, advert in the press. 'Only dial 999… if the matter is urgent; if, for instance, the man in the flat next to yours is murdering his wife or you have seen a heavily masked cat burglar peering round the stack pipe of the local bank building.'

THATCHER – MILK SNATCHER!

She smashed through the glass ceiling to become Britain's first female prime minister, she liberated the Falklands, broke the unions and even declared that there was 'no such thing as society' (to *Women's Own* magazine, no less). But what single act of perceived meanness do most people of a certain age really remember Mrs Thatcher for?

On 14 June 1971 Mrs T, then Education Secretary, was backed by 33 of her colleagues to slash spending in schools. Most controversially she planned to abolish free school milk for the over-sevens. Free milk for kids was a right enshrined in the 1946 Free School Milk Act and actually one of Churchill's ideas. British playgrounds rang with pint-size chants of 'Thatcher, Thatcher, Milk Snatcher!' – and she was never able to shake off the stigma.

But Downing Street meeting minutes reveal that the then newly politicised eight-year-olds were being a little unfair. Mrs Thatcher had, in fact, advised against cutting free school milk – predicting, correctly, the reaction. It would, she said in a memo, 'arouse widespread public antagonism'. Instead, she proposed charges for borrowing library books, museum entrance fees and hikes in school meal prices – also likely to be unpopular but less sensitively targeted.

The cuts were driven by the spectacularly poor outlook for the economy in the early 1970s. Edward Heath was returned to power that year and he knew he would have to make drastic cuts to fulfil the promises he made on tax during the election. A £200 million package of savings (almost £2 billion in today's money) – including the end to free milk and a hike in school meal prices – was passed by Heath to Thatcher for her to announce, and this sealed her reputation in the playground.

Many primary schools make milk available – although parents have to pay for it – and the under-fives in nursery and reception classes still have a state entitlement to it. Mindful of Thatcher's (alright, Heath's) divisive cuts, the former Tory PM David Cameron shot down a junior minister's suggestion that the public purse might benefit by cancelling milk for tots.

THE MATHS OF LIFE

MAKING A FIST OF THINGS

Throughout history there have been many ways to solve an argument. Sorting things out with a punch up or a shoot-out has always been popular. But there's an equally ancient, and less bloody, go-to issue solver. The game of Rock, Paper, Scissors. Played with three simple hand gestures, the premise is that – Rock blunts Scissors, Scissors cut Paper and Paper covers Rock; the game transcends language, religion and culture, and is played the world over.

It's known as Janken in Japan, and Japanese businessman Takashi Hashiyama famously used the game to solve a business conundrum.

Mr Hashiyama wanted to auction his company's $20 million art collection, which included a rare Van Gogh and an early Picasso. However, he couldn't pick between the equally respectable auction houses of Christie's and Sotheby's.

So he informed both auction houses that they would have one move each in a game of Janken, and the winner would be given the sale. The winning auction house could expect to make millions from the sales fees, so this was a proposition that need to be taken seriously.

Sotheby's decided to allow fate to guide their hand.

However, Kanae Ishibashi, the President of Christie's in Japan, decided to consult the experts, his colleague's twin 11-year-old daughters.

The girls pointed out that Rock would always feel like an obvious choice to start with. So in order to counter this, the opponent would most likely start with Paper. Therefore, they advised, you should always start with Scissors.

When it came to the fist-pumping battle royale, Sotheby's, as predicted by the tweenies, rolled out Paper while Christies, sticking to the advice, played Scissors – and scooped over £10 million in sales fees.

So is the secret of winning Rock, Paper, Scissors simply to stick to the Scissors option and wait for your opponent to slip up? Nope. Christie's were just lucky. In fact the more predictable you are – i.e. if you always play Scissors – the more you'll lose in the long run.

Dr Roman Belavkin from Middlesex University is an expert in game theory, the mathematical study of decision-making. Roman believes the minimax theorem, aka the Nash equilibrium, holds the answer to acing the game. (The Nash here, by the way, is John Nash, the Nobel-winning mathematician famously portrayed by Russell Crowe in the film *A Beautiful Mind*.) Roman explains:

> Minimax means you are trying to minimise your loss against a maximally capable opponent. There are two conditions for this solution. The first condition is you should play unbiased

strategies. Unbiased means in the game you should play Rock, Paper and Scissors with equal probability. If you play any one hand more frequently than the others, your opponent will beat you in the long run by changing strategy and using more of the trumping hand.

The mimimax theorem acknowledges that Rock, Paper or Scissors are all equally good choices. Each has one hand it can beat, one it can draw against and one against which it will lose. 'The key,' says Roman 'is ensuring you play them in a random order so your opponent can't predict what's coming next. But that can prove difficult because if you notice that you are losing you'll try to adjust and you will break independence.'

There is a counterintuitive way of not breaking your independence. Avoid second-guessing (which is only human but useless) by keeping your eyes closed. *The One Show* conducted a random experiment to illustrate this. Two teams of nine volunteers – Team A and Team B – were asked to play two lots of 936 games of RPS against each other. In the first session the teams could see each other and that, of course, would eventually influence their moves. Team A won 271 times, drew 345 times and lost 320 times. In the second session Team A wore blindfolds to help them utilise the minimax theorem. Now it was more difficult to be influenced by their opponents' moves and Team A won 327 times, drew 306 times and lost 303 times.

So if you have to decide who gets to auction a multi-million pound art collection or, more likely, who gets to pick up the bar tab, remember, don't trust an 11-year-old's opinion. Use the Nash equilibrium and keep your eyes shut.

MATHS AT THE POINTY END

In 1978 the beer-swilling, cigarette-smoking pub athletes of darts pierced the hearts and minds of the nation when the game became a TV fixture. Viewing figures in the early 1980s regularly topped ten million. The lifestyle choices of players were part of the package of darts; it enhanced the atmosphere of watching a game of 'arras', which was, after all, forged in the backstreet boozers of Britain. But as the decade progressed, social attitudes to both drinking and fitness had moved on considerably. As the bellies and drinking prowess of darts players became bigger news than the matches, viewers were switching off in droves.

The late 1980s and early '90s were fallow years for the sport. Today darts is enjoying a TV renaissance, but things have changed. Players may no longer be seen drinking on camera.

And the way the coverage is shot has changed too. It has created backroom stars from the dart spotters who employ maths and memory in equal measure.

Dart spotters are responsible for predicting where a dart player is going to aim before they even throw, so that the TV camera operators can get those great close-ups of darts hitting their targets.

Before the dart spotter, the camera operator either filmed the whole board or simply had to guess themselves, meaning that a lot of shots of the dart hitting the board for a specific score were missed and had to be shown on a much less engaging wide shot.

Keith Deller was the first champion who went on to become a professional spotter. He says:

Sky was just starting up its darts coverage, and I was still very much playing as a top professional player. They asked me if I would like to try spotting a match, because they wanted to get some really close-up shots of the darts hitting the board, and they needed someone who was able to guess where the player was going to throw. That's how it all began. I ended up playing and spotting at the same time for over 12 years.

So, how does a match work? 'Each player has to score 501 points in order to "check out" and win the match,' explains Keith. 'They have to either score a double or hit a bull's-eye to make up the final part of their score.' The spotter anticipates what score the player is going to go for. 'For the first two sets of three darts that they throw, they will usually be aiming to score a triple 20, making 60, which is the highest score in darts.'

Anticipating what the players will throw when they're nearing the end of the score – the 501 'checkout' – is where the skill of the spotter really comes to the fore. They have to be incredibly adept at fast mental arithmetic in order to anticipate the shot the player will be about to make as they will have literally seconds to do so.

Things get a little trickier when there are two options for the checkout, says Keith.

The spotter actually advises two different camera operators at the same time, one of whom is covering the top 180° of the board and the other who is covering the bottom 180°. So the spotter gives two options depending on whether the player goes for the top or the bottom of the board. There's also a third camera operator following the eyes of the players so that the dart spotter has a better chance of using the player's eyeline to help guess where he or she is going to throw.

Darts champ Eric Bristow says that the best way to learn the dark arts of dart spotting is pretty straightforward.

You have to learn the different checkout options, they have to come to you first hand. The player is obviously going to try and get out in as few darts as possible, and the last dart has to either be a double or the bull's-eye. This narrows the options. So if they have a score of 110 left, they would aim for a treble 20 and a bull to finish. Or if they had a score of 95 left, they would throw for a treble 19 and a double 19.

Dart spotters have years of playing and scoring experience, so much that it seems to come naturally. It seems like a dark art to the uninitiated, but Eric has some advice: 'Watch a lot of darts. Play a lot of darts. And then watch a lot more darts.' Thanks, Eric.

But there's also a mental arithmetic tip that might come in handy. In order to work out what the player is going to go for next, focus on the last digit of their remaining score. You can then work out what different factors you need to get in order to make that number. So if their score was 144 remaining, you should focus on the 4. What treble will give you a four? A treble 18 will give you 54 points, meaning the rest is easy to work out because 144 minus 54 is 90. Darts requires that you finish on a double, so the player needs to get a treble 20 for another 60 points, leaving them with 30. So, to finish the game, they'll play for a double 15.

'WHO WILL DO HIGHWAY ROBBERY ON THE OCHE?'

So asked Sid Waddell, commentating legend. In darts, the line from which the player throws is known as the oche (pronounced 'cocky' without the 'c'). The word could be derived from *hocken*, the Old English verb for spitting. It seems that distance spitting competitions – where the combatants expectorated against each other from behind a line – were once a thing in British pubs. Or it could be derived from the Flemish *oche*, basically a line, or groove, drawn in the dirt. Be wary of pub historians who'll tell you that oche is a nineteenth-century Cockney corruption of Hockey (and Sons). They'll tell you that beer crates from the brewery – apparently based in the West Country – were laid three in a line to mark the distance between board and player, thus establishing the standardised distance for throwing a dart. There is, however, no compelling evidence that there ever was a brewery called Hockey and Sons. Who knows what an oche really is? Who cares? In these modern, know-it-all times, it's somehow reassuring that one of the last harbours of mystery left is the game of darts.

HANG ON, LADS

It's one of the most iconic endings in British cinema – the definitive cliffhanger. In the 1969 British classic *The Italian Job*, a gang of bank robbers seesaw over a precipice inside a Harrington Legionnaire bus - lives and loot hanging in the balance. Just before the credits roll, Michael Caine's Charlie

Croker utters the immortal words: 'Hang on a minute, lads – I've got a great idea...'

But what *was* that great idea? The film ends before we can find out.

The producer Michael Deeley thought up the ending on a mid-Atlantic flight.

> I liked the idea of the film not really ending because it might give us a chance to make a sequel if the film was successful. It was a very naughty thing to do because in one way the audience is furious and in another way they're actually quite amused by it.

The sequel never materialised, so fans were left guessing... until 2009, when an unlikely institution came to the rescue. The Royal Society of Chemists ran a competition to find a theory that would save the gang and the gold; the winner was IT manager John Godwin.

'He'd really done his research, it was so thorough,' explains Lizzy Ratcliffe from the Society. 'It was about eight pages of workings and the maths and the engineering all checks out, so it's scientifically sound and it's very creative as well.'

The gist of Godwin's plan involved smashing the back windows of the Legionnaire, letting the air out of its front tyres, draining the fuel and allowing one person to leave. That (strong) person could then pass some loose rocks into the coach, anchoring it to the road and allowing the gold to be retrieved and the rest of the gang to escape.

Problem solved – though it might not make for the most riveting sequel in film history. Unsurprisingly Michael Deeley had a different solution, one that he'd previously explained to studio bosses at Paramount since it would be the opening scene of the next film.

> When you cut outside you see two helicopters, linked by a lowered cable. And the two helicopters come towards the back of the bus, hook up underneath the bus, lift up, and Bob's your uncle, it goes straight onto the ground. And out they all climb… and there's the Mafia. Our version was better. And true. It's the real version.

So there you have it, forget your forensic levels of mathematical detail, you were only supposed to helicopter the bloody bus to safety!

WHAT ARE THE CHANCES?

Would you believe that Roy Sullivan from Virginia was struck by lightning seven times and lived to tell the tale? Or that Joan Ginther from Texas has won the lottery four times? Or that Mark Twain was born shortly after Halley's Comet appeared in 1835 and died the day after it returned in 1910?

Think it's just the Americans who have a monopoly on bizarre coincidences? Think again. In Britain a chance encounter involving two young girls, a red balloon and a seemingly impossible set of coincidences would cause mathematicians to question the very nature of probability.

For reasons that will soon become clear, we'll let 'Laura Buxton 1' (LB1) explain what happened.

I was almost ten years old at the time and living in Stoke-on-Trent. My grandfather bought me a red balloon and asked me to write a note on a piece of paper that he attached to the balloon with string. He said that I might find a pen pal by sending the balloon with my name and address on it.

LB1 followed her grandfather's instructions, went out into her garden and released the balloon. 'We were laughing because we just thought it would get stuck in a tree or something.'

Here's where the balloon's recipient comes in.

Well, I was ten at the time and living about 140 miles south of Laura in a little place called Milton Lillbourne and the balloon landed in my hedge. My nextdoor neighbour found the balloon and was about to throw it away when he noticed the name and decided he should 'return' it to me. Yes, my name is also Laura Buxton.

LB2 decided to write back and it soon became apparent that the coincidences didn't end there.

Our parents were amazed! What were the chances? They arranged for us to meet up and that's when things only got weirder. We both had a three-year-old black Labrador, we both had a pet bunny and we both had a pet guinea pig (which we had both brought to the meeting without having talked to the other first), as well as both wearing pink jumpers and blue jeans.

The two Lauras have stayed in touch and remain friends to this day, a happy ending to this unlikely encounter.

Coincidences like the story of the two Lauras connected by the chance flight of a single balloon can seem so extraordinary, magical even. But is mathematical fact stranger than fiction? Professor David Hand is a leading statistician at Imperial College London, and can explain some of the maths behind these mystifying goings on. 'There are mysterious forces at work, but they're not mystical or magical. They are the forces of statistics and probability. They come from the mathematics underlying chance itself.'

Professor Hand is talking about 'the law of truly large numbers'.

Obviously there's only a tiny probability that one Laura Buxton would pick up a balloon launched by another Laura Buxton. But there's also a tiny probability that one John Smith would pick up a balloon launched by another John Smith. And a tiny probability that one Harold James would pick up a balloon launched by another Harold James. And so on. Factor in the number of balloon races in the UK each year, and the number of people who launch balloons at those races, and you're soon reaching a quite high chance that a balloon would be found by someone with the same name as the person who launched it.'

To further deflate us, Professor Hand concludes, 'We should also remember that it wasn't actually Laura who found the balloon but her neighbour and it's therefore even less of a coincidence than at first glance.'

There's another mathematical theory that also shows just how counterintuitive probability can be. It's called the birthday paradox and it tell us how many people there would have to be in a room for it to be more likely than not that two of them will share the same birthday (day and month).

You might think that you'd need 183 people to be confident of success (since that's just over a half of 365), but in any group of 23 people there is a 50 per cent chance that two of them will indeed share a birthday. Try it for yourselves. Fill a room with about 30 strangers and wager that two of them will have the same birthday. Then enjoy their amazement as your prophecy is proven correct. It could be the party trick you've always been looking for, or just get you locked up for bothering innocent members of the public.

Problems like the birthday paradox help us realise that coincidences, such as a toy balloon flying 225 km (140 miles) from one Laura Buxton to another, are in fact simply proofs of probability. That doesn't mean we shouldn't enjoy them, though...

STARS TURNING UP IN STRANGE PLACES

FRANK WHO?

Singer Frank Sinatra began his career with the Tommy Dorsey Orchestra, but in 1942 his decision to go solo made him a star. Within a year the unrivalled popularity of his live performances had won him a film deal. By 1945 he was one of the biggest stars in Hollywood.

So why was it that just eight years later, when Sinatra came to Britain for a 50-date tour, he played to theatres that were all but empty?

1953 was not Frank Sinatra's year – he'd probably describe it as a swingin' *annus horribilis*. His divorce from the actress Ava Gardner had been messy, and while it was her infidelity that was blamed, Sinatra bore the brunt of widespread public disapproval. Publicly he was brazen about the divorce, privately he'd made two serious attempts to end his life. That same year a second front on Sinatra's reputation opened. US newspapers began circulating rumours that the singing star was linked to Mafia crime bosses. Little wonder he readily agreed to a European tour.

But scandal knows no borders. During the Scandinavian leg, crowds took the moral high ground and stayed away in droves, forcing Sinatra to cancel most of the dates. Things, surely, would be different in the UK? Sinatra was an Anglophile and his record sales suggested Britain was likewise enamoured.

Not so. The tour bombed.

So what had gone so terribly wrong?

Professor Carol Smart of the University of Manchester is an expert in the social morals and foibles of the times. 'Attitudes towards divorce back then were negative, to say the least. It simply wasn't the done thing. Marriage, church and thus religion were inexorably intertwined. There was a lot of stigma attached to divorce and divorcees in the public eye were viewed as especially deviant.'

Two decades before, a divorcée – Wallis Simpson – had been the catalyst of the abdication of King Edward VIII, which shocked the nation. Wallis was vilified in the UK. When Group Captain Peter Townsend, also divorced, proposed to Princess Margaret in 1952, there were fears that history was repeating itself and the relationship soon fizzled out under pressure. Townsend was sent to be the diplomatic attaché in Belgium. Punishment indeed.

Sinatra fell prey to the same moral rigidity.

It went to show just how steadfast attitudes were, it was a scandal. Establishment attitudes towards divorce and remarriage were pretty vehement, there was a sense that it was becoming fashionable among celebrities and there was a fear that the trend would be picked up by ordinary people. The country had just come through the Second World War, the mindset of the time was that people wanted stability. The idea of happiness through consumption had begun, this idea of the perfect house with the perfect family, and I think having a rich and famous celebrity like Sinatra basically saying he didn't believe in or need that was a real threat to those ideals.

It's worth noting that the press reserved the sharpest criticism for divorcées, like Wallis Simpson and Ava Gardner. But Frank still must have felt like somebody had drawn a big target on top of his trademark trilby (not, as commonly believed, a fedora – there *is* a difference, but this isn't a story about hats, so you'll just have to trust me). In every town he played, promoters complained about the wads of unsold tickets.

The beautiful and retitled Birmingham Hippodrome, opened in 1903 with 2,000 seats, was typical of the cavernous British venues into which Sinatra was booked. Expecting the screams of thousands of bobby soxers – the Beliebers or Directioners of the era, identified by their hysterical screaming, ponytails, poodle skirts and bobby socks rolled down to the ankle and worn under Penny Loafer shoes – Sinatra instead heard the reverb of his own voice, bouncing back at him from the far end of the hall.

Roy Edwards was there, though. And he'll never forget it. Ray was 20 in 1953 and Frank Sinatra was – still is – his idol.

I'd bought a ticket in advance, which was unusual at the time, really. Usually you could just get a ticket on the door for most shows. But this was Sinatra, he was a big star, so I thought

I'd better get a ticket in advance. I was sat in the circle and I couldn't believe it, there was hardly anyone there. The stalls in front of the stage were completely empty.

Sinatra walked on stage to be greeted with desultory applause.

He looked out at the auditorium and he put his hand to his forehead and he said, 'Is there anybody out there?' A few of us shouted 'yes' and he said, 'Come on down and sit at the front.' We gathered at the front of the stage near the front rows.

So intimate was the following performance that Frank even took requests. Roy asked for 'Ol' Man River'. 'It was a big thrill to hear him doing that number, to actually see Frank performing it. It's hard to describe today what the thrill was to see somebody like that, so close.'

After making the best of things on stage, Sinatra could be forgiven for seeking the solace of a pint in the nearest pub – which is what he did. Roy Edwards, who'd left the show in a considerably lighter mood than Frank, had got to the boozer ahead of Frank.

I'd just left the gig and met a friend for a drink, we'd ordered a pint, and taken a seat, when the whole pub went quiet. I turned around and Sinatra just walked in with his entourage, and ordered a drink. He was literally six feet away. He took the drink and went through to a backroom.

To be in such close proximity to his hero twice in the same night was almost too much for Roy. 'It was absolutely amazing to see him there in the bar, but I didn't have the nerve to go and talk to him!'

1953, then, was not, to paraphrase one of the singer's later hits, 'a very good year'. Amid divorce and mobster rumours, his record label Columbia signed Eddie Fisher (the father of the late actress Carrie) and gave *him* all the hits originally penned with Frank in mind. Then Frank's US TV show was axed.

But at his lowest ebb his fortunes began to recover. Earlier that same year he had played a supporting role in *From Here to Eternity*. Within a year, he won an Oscar for that performance and was being lined up for more lucrative roles including the fondly remembered, but let's be honest, largely rubbish, Rat Pack films. Recording-wise he soon trounced Eddie Fisher with a string of excellent singles and albums. And while the rumours about his personal life and even the underworld never really dissipated, Sinatra concentrated on his peerless voice; he was a tough man who'd lived and learned his entire life.

JACKSON 5 ASIDE

In 2002 Michael Jackson, the King of Pop, was made an honorary director of Exeter City Football Club by his old pal, and co-chairman and director of the club, Uri Geller – the spoon-bending, psychic Israeli. This was just the latest bizarre incident involving Geller's strange obsession with the struggling Devon team.

Some years before he took to the boardroom at Exeter, Geller assisted the club by planting a batch of psychically charged crystals behind Exeter's goals at the team's ground, St

James Park. Geller buried them in earnest, in order to hurtle Exeter forward to victory over Chester in a Division Three playoff in April 1997.

Exeter lost 5–1.

Don't be too hasty to write off Geller as a complete fraud – or, indeed, crystal magic as equally fake. After all, from where Chester fans were standing the enterprise was entirely successful in repeatedly drawing the ball to Exeter's goal. If Geller had remembered that the rules of professional football require the teams to swap direction in the second half he could have done a spot of half-time gardening. At the least he might have evened things up by planting magic rocks at both goal ends.

Anyway… some five years later Geller returned to Exeter to become a director, his son Daniel being appointed vice-chairman. The cash-strapped club hoped that Geller's fame, celebrity associations – and money – would draw other investors. Geller's explanation was, typically, more fanciful. His interest in Exeter was, he said, because of a psychic vision, which revealed to him that Daniel had lived in the Devonshire city during the witch hunts of the seventeenth century.

The Football Association's guidelines for directors do not have any stipulations or clauses about the reincarnations or past lives of club directors (unless they have an undeclared criminal conviction or bankruptcy), so Daniel's position on the board was all above board. However, directors of football clubs *are* required to register with Companies House, and neither Uri nor his son had done so. Because of this oversight the pair were obliged to temporarily stand down from the role in 2003. One might wonder how a psychic, with or without knowledge of corporate law, didn't see that coming. Either way it coincided with more bad news when Exeter were relegated to the game's graveyard shift: the Football Conference league. Not long after that, Uri gave up his position for good.

So, Geller's name on Exeter's books – like his crystals under the goal posts – didn't make much of a difference to the club's fortunes. But he did create one unforgettable moment at St James when he got out his address book and started hammering the telephone to put together a dream team of celebs to raise money for Exeter City – including David Blaine and, er, Patti Boulaye (a pop singer who hadn't worried the charts in a while).

Topping the bill, and generating an enormous amount of publicity on the day (described as a 'circus' by the Reuters press agency) was none other than Michael Jackson. Jackson didn't perform any hits, he just sort of waved and mumbled a speech. But still, it *was* Michael Jackson and *this* was Exeter. There are Exeter City fans of a certain vintage who to this day tell their younger compatriots about the time Michael Jackson came to St James. Invariably the reply is 'Michael who?' followed by 'Exeter has a football team?'

Geller rewarded Michael with an honorary directorship of the club. This entitled the King of Pop to lord it up in boardroom conferences and vote on key decisions about the squad. He was also permitted to travel with the players on the coach to any away game he wanted to. It should come as no surprise, but is nonetheless disappointing, that Jackson never took the opportunity to fulfil any of those duties. But when he visited the club for the charity event he still came with slightly different demands those of a prospective striker from Grimsby: he asked for his dressing room to be filled with flowers and for it to be kept at the exact temperature of 23°C (74°F) for the duration of his visit.

A (BLONDE) BOMBSHELL GOES OFF IN LEEDS

Jayne Mansfield was for a time amongst the most famous actresses on the planet. The studios billed her as the working man's Monroe and she starred in box office hits like *The Girl Can't Help It* (1956), one of the first films to cash in on the rock and roll craze, and *Promises Promises* (1963). But by 1967 Hollywood had grown tired of Jayne's limited acting range and the public of her publicity stunts – which usually involved her revealing her ample bosom. Jayne was, if not on her uppers, certainly in need of a cash injection what with the film roles drying up, a third divorce that wasn't going her way and five children to support.

Remembering the success she'd enjoyed in previous visits to the UK – turning on the Blackpool illuminations, opening the Chiswick flyover and being trodden on by an elephant to advertise Billy Smart's circus, among them – the blonde bombshell was delighted to accept an invitation to take to the stages of the North of England's most famous clubs. That invitation came from pop impresario Don Arden – manager of the Small Faces and, perhaps more famously, dad of Sharon Osborne. Don just knew Jayne still had pulling power.

From La Dolce Vita in Newcastle to La Bamba in Darlington and The Latino in South Shields – Mansfield played them all. And while she may have fallen on hard times, and northern clubs are a little more 'real', certainly 'earthier' than the venues of the world's capitals she had once known, she was still every inch a star. The BBC documentary strand *24 Hours* followed her for part of the tour to see for themselves the American interpretation of 'doing a turn': 'Whatever her reception she never needs to feel lonely. Moral support comes from her American road manager, her British road manager, her hairdresser, her showbiz agent and her impresario advisor.'

Surely the most famous, most prestigious of all the northern clubs, though, was the Batley Variety Club – known as the Las Vegas of the North – and situated in Batley, near Leeds. Her fee for the week? £4,000, or a cool £25,000 in today's money.

Carl Gresham handled the club's press and publicity at the time.

> She was this icon in Hollywood and she had this aura. She walked on the stage and people immediately went, '*This* is what we have come to see.' Then she would walk down off the stage and would find a lovely table that had ladies and gentlemen on and she would sit on one of the men's knees and you could see the seething anger of the girls, their wives, thinking, 'What is she going to do now?'

What Mansfield *did* do next was find a truly captive audience without any wives to offend. She invited the press to see her in concert at probably *the* ultimate working men's club – Leeds Prison. Entertainer Les Piggen shared the bill.

> She was introduced by the chaplain, she let the applause die down a bit, let them settle. Then she said, looking at them

straight and knowing exactly what she was saying. 'Would you like to see my Chihuahuas?' It was tremendous, the whole prison was in *uproar*. She let the wolf whistles die down, gave a signal and out came a liveried chauffer with these two little dogs... her Chihuahuas.

Ten years earlier Jayne had won a Golden Globe in Hollywood as Most Promising Actress. Now she was dropping cheap double entendres in a British prison to pay for the maintenance of her children. Having hit the bottom career-wise, Jayne believed that she could put it down to experience. Once back home in the States she could take a breath and then start to reinvent her act... and herself.

She didn't get the opportunity, though. She'd barely been home a month when she was involved in a terrible car crash on Highway 90, east of New Orleans, Louisiana. Jayne Mansfield died on 29 June 1967.

During the BBC documentary made during her tour of Yorkshire, the interviewer asked Jayne how long she thought she would remain a sex symbol.

'Forever,' she answered, with a giggle.

Sadly, her death ensured that she would.

NEVER MIND THE HORLICKS... MUHAMMAD ALI SAYS, "DRINK OVALTINE". OR ELSE!

On 19 October 1971 thousands of people gathered outside the T. W. Downs supermarket in the St Stephen's district of Norwich. They had arrived en masse for an instore event promoting Ovaltine. If you are under 60 or not convalescing after a serious illness, Ovaltine is a malt and powdered-egg concoction developed in Switzerland in 1904. Once mixed into hot milk, it is drunk as an overture to a good night's sleep. Ovaltine is easily confused with the rival powdered malt drink Horlicks; they taste similar and are believed to have the same pre-bedtime calming powers. But Horlicks is of slightly earlier origin and is a British product – although its inventor was resident in the United States before moving production to Slough.

Norwich has long suffered the accusation that it is one of the less stimulating of the UK's provincial cities. That such a sizable cross-section of the city's population turned out for a 'one day only' discount on a powdered malt drink might seem to confirm that slur. But it wasn't the promotion they'd gathered for; it was the promoter. None other than the most famous sports personality on the planet at the time: Muhammed Ali.

Why he was in Norwich involves quite a back story, so make yourself comfortable. Perhaps with a hot malted milk?

In 1964 Muhammad Ali, then known as Cassius Clay, won his first World Heavyweight title against the 'unbeatable' Charles 'Sonny' Liston. Until then Clay had been massively underrated by the boxing establishment, and as Clay put it himself, his win 'shook up the world'.

Clay was an outstanding boxer, but he was also an outstanding character. Eloquent, principled, intellectual and very funny, he was never afraid to speak his mind or stand up for his beliefs. He was a champion of the underdog because he'd been the underdog and it was this rare common touch that won him millions of admirers – boxing fans or not. He was famous for his outrageous bragging, reminding the world at every opportunity that he was 'the greatest' (and, on more than one occasion in the ring, he absolutely was), but he wore a heart as big as his fists on his sleeve and people loved him for it.

Clay had become interested in Islam prior to his fight with Liston and converted to the faith a little after in 1964. That year, he changed his name to Muhammad Ali, asserting that 'Cassius Clay was my slave name.'

In 1967, with the Vietnam War raging, Ali took a stance and refused to be drafted into the US Army. He said that he had no argument with the Viet Cong (the communist-backed combatants fighting the USA), and he highlighted the hypocrisy that demanded a disproportionate number of young African-Americans enlisted to fight a war for a country that denied their civil rights on almost every level.

The US press and establishment thought Ali had betrayed the nation. The boxing authorities stripped him of the World Heavyweight title and revoked his boxing licence, leaving Ali chastised, unable to compete in the ring and banned from foreign travel.

In the UK, Ali's admirers, black and white, were shocked by his treatment and continued to support him – a fact, he said, he was touched by and which he always appreciated.

By 1970, US public opinion towards the Vietnam War had changed. Rather than being seen as a pariah, Ali was viewed by the public as a principled spokesperson for a generation. The boxing authorities buckled and reinstated Ali's boxing licence. Muhammad Ali was now able to get a shot at reclaiming his title. But it didn't go to plan.

In March 1971, his title challenge against his greatest rival Joe Frazier ended in defeat and so did his dreams of reversing his fortune. He needed to earn a living, but at least he was still

a big enough name to endorse products. These were unenlight-
ened times and Ali was being offered gigs to hustle alcohol and
tobacco – a complete no-no considering his faith. But then he
received a call from the UK wondering if Muhammad Ali had
ever heard of Ovaltine.

Ovaltine had an image problem. It was a bedtime drink
associated with the 1940s and consumers had pushed it to the
back of the cupboard. Ovaltine wanted someone who screamed
– literally – 1970s cool, and Ali's sporting loss became their
gain. And so Ali was hired for a short series of appearances
across the UK to promote the drink's vitality-giving properties.

Ali arrived in Norwich by train to be greeted by hundreds of
fans. Even more turned out to see their hero at the supermarket.

With so many people trying to get a glimpse of arguably
the most famous man in sport, Ali's security team needed some
local help. Former boxer Les King was a bouncer at Norwich's
Washington Club 400 (then the city's only club offering entertainment past 11 p.m.) and he was tasked with escorting Ali
from the station to the supermarket. 'The Manager of T.W.
Downs supermarket was one of our customers at the 400
Club. He told me that Muhammad Ali was going to be signing
autographs and he needed some security. He knew that I boxed
and was a huge fan, so how could I say no?'

So it was that Les found himself on the security detail of
possibly the least likely man in the world in need of protection.

He arrived in a black limousine and my job was to make
sure he got to the rear entrance of the supermarket safely.
There were fans everywhere, thousands of them, it was pretty
daunting. When Ali got out his car, I could not believe the

size of him, he towered over everyone. We guided him to the rear entrance and walked him up to the Ovaltine display. You could hear all the fans chanting his name. There was so much excitement and thankfully no trouble. He shook my hand and said, 'Thank you'. He was so generous and humble, but you knew he could put you on the floor in a second. A great man. Like he said, the greatest.

Quite.

Peter Smith was 16 years old at the time. He idolised Ali and was desperate to get close to him. Which happened to be everybody else's plan, too. 'Norwich had never seen nothing like that, it was crazy,' laughs Pete, four-and-a-half decades on.

We're standing there with all the old ladies with their head scarves on, pushing and jostling, everybody wants Ali to sign their tin of Ovaltine. I'm there with my mate Mickey Romanos. Mickey's nose is a bit squashed like a boxer's – you'd think he was a boxer if you saw him – and when we see Ali we're trying to get his attention. I'm shouting, 'Alright, Ali… hey, Muhammad' and he must have seen us because he stopped and looked at Mickey, probably thought he was a boxer like everyone else did because of his nose, and then suddenly Ali sends out a jab. His knuckle stops less than a quarter of an inch away from his nose, really precise; and then we all start laughing and Ali starts doing that famous boxing shuffle with us and pretends to spar.

Moments later a BBC reporter asked Pete what he thought Ali's chance would be in an upcoming return bout against his nemesis Joe Frazier. 'This time,' the young Pete predicts on camera, 'he's going to beat him.' It's a treasured memory for Pete to this day, 'and I was right – he did beat him.' And Ali would go on to beat Frazier yet again in a now legendary bout, the Thrilla In Manilla. 'It was an incredible moment for me, to see him up close in Norwich,' says Pete, 'I shook the hand that rocked the world.'

Ali, uncharacteristically bashful, told reporters that he was overwhelmed by the reception he'd received in Norwich.

When you live in the USA you think of England and you think of London, but coming here I've met the most civilised people around. I never would have had no reason to come here if it wasn't for working with Ovaltine. And I'm glad of that because I never realised how many people I had following me.

As a parting gesture to the people of Norwich Muhammad reeled off one of his now trademark raps: 'I like Ovaltine, and I like your style, but your pants are so cheap, I won't be back for a while.'

Ali never did return to Norwich, but the city will never forgot him.

AND NOW... FROM NORWICH

By happy coincidence, Muhammed Ali's visit to Norwich in October 1971 marked the second time that month that the city had been associated with a culture phenomenon. *Sale of the Century*, one of ITV's most popular gameshows of the 1970s and early '80s, launched on 9 October 1971, recorded in front of a live audience from Anglia TV's studios in Norwich. Presented by Nicholas Parsons – whose manner with contestants was not dissimilar to the slightly peeved headmaster of a minor public school – the show announced its presence each episode with the (soon to be affectionately mocked) voiceover: 'And now... from Norwich... it's the quiz of the week!".

Sale of the Century was originally planned just for the Anglia TV region, but by 1975 had been syndicated across the nation with each ITV region transmitting it at times that suited them – usually in the afternoon or early evening. It's easy to mock now (there are plenty of great clips on YouTube), but *Sale of the Century* revolutionised the British gameshow format. Taking its cue from US gameshows, it was flashy, aspirational (just listen to Peter Fenn's kitschy theme tune, called 'Joyful Pete') and offered extravagant prizes such as a family car, a hair dryer or a wardrobe of new clothes.

In fact, contestants had to answer questions to win money to pay for very heavily discounted goods (the Sale of the Century, you see?) rather than prizes. But splitting hairs aside, these far outvalued and outclassed anything being offered by rival shows – to the point that early in its history the producers were criticised by media regulators for promoting lifestyles that were unachievable for most of the people viewing.

What the producers spent on top-shelf goods, though, they saved on their studio audience's bottoms. For the first series of the show, at least, audience members are seated on

what are clearly Polypropylene Eco Chairs. This uncomfortable but classic 1970s utility chair was designed for stacking
and, until its moment of TV stardom, was more familiar to
school kids and organisers of church hall meetings.

WALT DISNEY DOESN'T LIVE HERE ANYMORE

In spite of what Mickey and co might tell you, the world's first
documented mention of Disneyland was not referring to the
American theme park that opened in Anaheim, California, on
17 July 1955. It was written on a twelfth-century English deed
denoting the ownership of a muddy field, and some woods, in
rural Lincolnshire.

But there *is* a connection between the two, which explains
why, in 1949, Walt Disney himself rolled up in the sleepy village
of, well, Norton Disney.

Many Disney films – *One Hundred and One Dalmatians*,
The Rescuers, *Finding Nemo* – are about the search for family.
And when, in 1949, Walt Disney came to visit Norton Disney
and have a rifle through the parish records, it was in part to
prove to himself he had a heritage. Walt had no birth certificate
and the only official record of a Walter Disney in the United
States was dated a decade before Walt could have been born.
The idea that Walt had been adopted was a source of gossip
in the press, which hurt Walt's feelings.

His childhood had been tough in places, due to his family's
lack of money and his father's stern nature, but Walt was
definitely not adopted. Born to Elias and Flora, he was one of
five children, and a Disney through and through. Now, since
he was in the UK (overseeing *Treasure Island*, the studio's first

live action feature), he decided to celebrate with a visit to his ancestral home.

Disney is an anglicised version of the French *D'Isigny* – literally 'of Isigny'. Isigny is a hamlet near Bayeux, the town famous for its stitched early comic strip – or, as traditionalists prefer, tapestry – and the D'Isignys arrived in England as soldiers of fortune with William the Conqueror in the eleventh century. Paid in land for their loyalty, they established a manor and a church about 24 km (15 miles) from Lincoln. The village prospered and by the thirteenth century their name had become Disney. In the late seventeenth century, the Disneys took part in a failed rebellion against the king, were kicked out of England, settled in Ireland and, sometime in the nineteenth century, emigrated to America.

When Walt visited in July 1949, he recorded as much as he could on his own cine-camera. He met starstruck locals in the village, had a drink in the St. Vincent Arms (now called The Green Man – which still has pictures of the visit) and spent an hour in the church looking at medieval tombs inscribed with the word Disney – proving the family had a knack for branding long before Mickey Mouse popped out of Walt's head. It was also here that Walt was given access to the parish records and pored over ancient documents pertaining to his ancestors. Among those was a sheet of vellum detailing the ownership of outlying fields, including a group of plots described collectively as Disneyland.

Whether Walt found some real closure on his sentimental journey is not clear. However, his corporation could never be accused of being dewy-eyed. Family or not, anyone hoping to register the name Disney as a business will receive short shrift. In the early 2000s a locally run hotel and business centre opened for business and registered itself as the Norton Disney Conference Centre. Disney in the USA took umbrage and had their lawyers send a cease and desist letter. The owners thought that Disney were taking the Mickey. They weren't and the centre is now called Norton Lodge.

THE TERMINATOR IN ILFORD

The man known variously as the Austrian Oak, The Terminator, The Governator or, simply, Arnie started along his extraordinary career path here in the UK. Losing out in the 1966 Mr Universe Competition at the tender age of 19 (because his calves weren't defined enough), Arnie was taken under the wing of one of the judges, a former bodybuilder. Charles 'Wag' Bennett was an East Ender, who lived and owned a body building gym in Forest Gate, East London.

Charles and his wife Dianne took in Arnie because they could see his potential and also because they felt a bit sorry for the hulking Austrian (with the skinny calves). Arnie slept on a sofa on and off for a number of years whilst training at Charles' gym and working on his bodybuilding career, and would listen to bedtime stories told to Charles, and Dianne's kids in the next room. When the stories stopped for any reason, he would stick his head through the hatch and inquire: 'But vot happened next?'

What happened next for Arnie is, of course, the stuff of legend: he defined his calves, won Mr. Universe, went to the USA and became Hollywood's highest paid star. But

he never forgot his formative years in the East End and he
stayed in contact with the Bennetts.

ALL YOU NEED IS DOVES

Pablo Picasso was one of the twentieth century's greatest
painters and sculptors. With three places in the Top 10 list of
the most expensive paintings of all time, he is matched only
by Van Gogh. Van Gogh died a pauper; Picasso, a millionaire.

Picasso lived variously in Paris and Barcelona and owned
villas in Mougins and the Cote d'Azur. In his lifetime, he visited
Britain only twice – once in 1919, to attend a performance
of Diaghilev's production of *Le Tricorne* for which he had
designed the costumes and sets, and a second time in 1950,
when the artist found himself in, of all places, Sheffield, the
steel capital of Britain, on a cold, grey day in November.

He had come to speak at the second International Peace
Conference having been an active advocate for peace since the
bombing of the Basque town of Guernica in 1937 – inspiring
his famous painting of the same name. Bill Romsley, now a
retired train driver, was one of the delegation that met Picasso
on the platform at the then Sheffield Midland station.

He arrived on platform one on the train from London, with
his bodyguard. He had an old overcoat on, a tweed suit, a
blue beret and was carrying a bunch of big-headed chrysan-
themums. He didn't really look like we'd expected, not a
millionaire at least. After we said hello we took him down
Thorpe's Café for a bacon sandwich.

Joan Brown was another Peace Conference delegate. 'The peace movement was so important to us then. You have to remember that we'd all just been through the Blitz. We didn't want to see it happen again, we wanted a new age of peace.' Hearing that Picasso had arrived, Joan, with her friend Chris, went to Thorpe's Café to share a sarnie with the artists. Chris, though, had an issue. 'He didn't have any teeth. And he was very self-conscious, especially meeting such a legend as Picasso, so he took a set of dentures along in his pocket, and just before he went up to him he popped them in so he could say hello.'

Joan remembers a feeling of disbelief that Picasso had deigned to support them; 'the feeling was that this would heap a lot of worldwide attention on what we were doing in Sheffield, so we were very proud'. Whilst he was there Picasso helped raise funds for the movement. 'He drew doves on paper napkins and sold one in the hall to the highest bidder to raise money for the cause. I really wanted it, but my husband and I didn't have any money to speak of and in the end it went to an American for £200' (about £6,500 in 2017).

After Picasso ate his bacon roll, he stopped by Peckitt's barbers for a trim, paying the barber with another drawing of a dove of peace. He gave his bodyguard another one of the napkin drawings of the dove of peace, which now resides in Sheffield's Weston Park Museum.

Then he made his way to Sheffield City Hall to be greeted by the press. Unfortunately the conference wasn't to be the great move to peace that had been planned.

The conference was arranged by the Communist Party, so visas to enter Britain were refused for many delegates, and the event had to be curtailed. However, Picasso still made a short speech to the small crowd that had assembled, and told them how his father had taught him to draw the dove and how he believed in peace, not war.

But with no conference to attend, what else was Pablo to do with his time in Britain? Spend time with some long-term friends in Sussex. Tony Penrose is the son of photographer Lee Miller and artist Roland Penrose, who Picasso first met in Paris in the 1930s. Although he was only a child at the time, he vividly remembers his first meeting with Picasso in 1950. 'I bit him!' grins Tony. 'We were playing in the garden – he was very playful and expressive, not at all the British style. We might have been playing bulls and bullfighters, I think, and at one point I bit him.' Pablo's response was to bite the toddler back, 'then he said in French, "It is the first Englishman I have ever bitten."' In spite of the violence it was the start of a fond relationship between Tony and Picasso.

> He was very warm and very supportive when I was growing up and was having a bad time at school. He would send me drawings – he sent one with a bull, a dancer and a centaur, and on the top he wrote 'Pour Tony'; that meant a huge amount to me. He was a great man.

On one level the International Peace Conference may not have achieved the potential its organisers planned, but just the presence of Picasso in the city gave Sheffield a real boost. Even today his visit is celebrated, and if you look closely you can see on top of the chimneys, above the city's Peace Gardens, steel doves inspired by Picasso's dove of peace.

DALI IN A DIVE SUIT

On 1 July 1936, Spanish artist Salvador Dali planned to give the lecture of a lifetime at the Surrealist exhibition in London. The show was the first of its kind in Britain and had attracted crowds large enough to bring the traffic in Piccadilly to a standstill. Ever the showman, Dali caused a furore by stepping onto the stage wearing a full deep-sea diving suit, carrying a billiard cue and leading a pair of Russian wolfhounds. When the eminent surrealist began to flail about, the audience thought it was part of the act and started cheering. In fact, Dali was suffocating. Luckily, he was prised out of the helmet with plyers by poet David Gascoyne and artist Edward James, who realised that their friend was in trouble. Dali always maintained that he wore the suit because he 'just wanted to show that I was plunging deeply into the human mind'. It nearly cost him his life.

ALL AROUND MAHATMA

Mohandas Gandhi, also known as Mahatma, meaning the 'high-souled', was famous the world over for promoting the creation of an Indian state – with Hindus and Muslims united, and independent of British rule. His tireless campaign of non-violent, civil disobedience led to him being arrested countless times over his lifetime, yet ultimately he was successful and India achieved independence in 1947.

Gandhi was no stranger to Britain and as a young man had studied law in London for ten years. During the struggle for independence, he returned for round-table discussions with a reluctant British government. But in the middle of his trip he got on a train and headed north, ending up in a small Lancashire industrial town called Darwen, on the evening of Friday, 26 September 1931.

Local historian Jane Waring explains why:

Darwen was one of scores of Lancashire cotton towns and was at the height of its production at the beginning of the twentieth century. The industry dominated the town and was by far the greatest employer. As part of the struggle for independence Gandhi encouraged Indians to boycott British goods, especially textiles, as Britain, through the British Empire, had largely destroyed India's industrialised cotton production through taxes and trade restrictions, to benefit the industry at home. They had returned to handlooms and Gandhi was encouraging fellow Indians to support their own market.

Thousands of miles away in England, that boycott resulted in the laying off of thousands of Lancashire millworkers.

Gandhi was invited to Darwen by a local welfare officer and peace protester called Corder Catchpool. Catchpool, a Quaker, admired Gandhi but wanted him to see the effects of the boycott in the town and across the region.

The local newspaper described Gandhi as having 'the legal eye and forehead – an eye as piercing as a rapier – of moderate physique and slender proportions… with the appearance of being rather tired.'

But there's a still-living witness who got a different view of

Gandhi. In 1931 Gusta Green was ten years old. She came to the centre of town to see Gandhi arrive. 'He stroked my cheek,' she remembers fondly.

> I already knew who he was. My father had a machinist's shop down the road at the time and he knew that Gandhi was going to be walking through town. He sat me down and told me that a very important man would be coming, that he meant a lot to a lot of people and one day he would be famous.

Gusta pushed her way through the crowd and saw history in the making.

> There was a big entourage that came with him, and I remember seeing these skinny legs and big shoes. He stopped in front of me, patted me on my head, stroked my cheek and grinned at my father – he didn't have many teeth, as I recall, just one or two.

Gandhi spent the whole visit dressed in his traditional robes and sandals, and in the afternoon he went to the Spring Vale area of Darwen to visit Greenfield Mill. The mill is no longer, but across the road is Spring Vale Gardens and the still standing terraces built by the mill's Quaker owners for the workers. Gandhi spent his first night in Darwen in No. 3. He was such a controversial figure that the police maintained a large presence around the house, but the workers of Darwen were sanguine about his visit. In fact he was, by and large, greeted with open arms.

The grandmother of councillor Eileen Entwistle was one of the workers at Greenfield Mill who met Gandhi.

Of course the mill workers resented the fact they were out of work, there's no two ways about it. Even when they were in work it was a very hard life for a mill worker then – you worked six days a week, and only had two weeks holiday in the year and the pay was very low. There was real poverty. But, of course, they also *knew* that Indian cotton weavers were as poor, even poorer, so there was also some solidarity; it was hard to be angry.

Gandhi was also a novelty, says Eileen. 'Back in the 1930s the furthest most mill workers would have ever travelled would be to Blackpool on holiday during Wakes Weeks. India may as well have been the moon. So yes, I imagine they found it very exciting and very exotic.'

Gandhi stayed the next night with the owners of Greenfield Mill, and took a long walk over the moors the following day before returning to London. The people of Darwen may have taken him to their hearts, but in the end the ultimate outcome of the visit didn't save the town. At the beginning of the twentieth century there were more than 79,000 looms in Darwen. By the end, there were none. Cheaper overseas labour changed the face of Lancashire forever.

Sixteen years after his visit, Gandhi did bring independence for India in August 1947, but at a price: the creation of the separate Islamic nation of Pakistan. Gandhi had not achieved what he so longed for – the unity of Hindus and Muslims – an in a violent backlash in January 1948 an extremist Hindu nationalist shot him dead. It was a desperately sad end.

But for one brief weekend, in the autumn of 1931, two worlds had met in Lancashire – both trying to secure a future for their people.

GREAT BRITISH ECCENTRICS

I CAN'T BELIEVE IT'S NOT BUDDHA

Today thousands of Britons have embraced the culture of Tibet, including its particular form of Buddhism. But in the 1950s few in Britain had ever even heard of the country.

That was all about to change in the strangest way. In 1951, a Tibetan monk called Tuesday Lobsang Rampa wandered into the London offices of publishers Secker & Warburg (the original publishers of *Animal Farm*) and delivered a book pitch so out-there it was greeted with slack-jawed silence.

Even by the standards of most of the writers who fetched up in the publisher's Bloomsbury offices, Lobsang Rampa was strange. He spoke with a squeaky voice and a West Country accent, and he didn't look particularly Tibetan. Still, it was a great story. He had, he explained, been born into monastic Buddhist life in the Himalayas.

Sometime between his sixth and his eighth birthday (he gave

differing dates) the monks identified him as 'the chosen one', the reincarnation of an ancient lama called Lobsang Rampa. A *lama* is a venerated Buddhist teacher, and the term has a meaning similar to the Sanskrit word *guru*.

Before he could achieve the absolute greatness that was his destiny, the boy would require a small surgical procedure: a hole, drilled into his skull. This type of operation is known as trepanning and it's an ancient practice; the skulls of cave-dwelling early humans have been discovered with scars that could only have been caused by trepanning. The practice may have developed as an early, and extreme, treatment for a range of ailments from schizophrenia to epilepsy – then only explainable as demonic possession. A hole in the head was the means of escape for whatever had taken up residence in one's head. But in Tibet, Lobsang told the enthralled publisher, the procedure was designed as some kind of enhancement to his human abilities. Parts of his brain were replaced with crystals and wood. This, he said, activated his 'third eye' and had the effect of turning him into a psychic aerial able to pick up visions and prophesies being beamed to him from the ether.

Later on in the pitch Lobsang related a snowy encounter with the Abominable Snowman – today more commonly known as the Yeti – and also described how he had chanced upon the mummified remains of his own body prior to being reincarnated.

As the meeting drew to a close, the incredulous publisher revealed that he actually knew a few words of Tibetan. He spoke them. Lobsang frowned and said he didn't understand the words but quickly gave an explanation. When the People's Republic of China aggressively incorporated Tibet in the late

1940s and early 1950s, Lobsang psychically wiped clean his brain so that he could not give away any sacred secrets to the aggressors. 'It's all in here,' he said, impatiently waving the manuscript of his book, *The Third Eye*.

'It was a wonderful tale,' says Charles Allen, author and historian of Buddhism,

> . . . exotic and strange – he said his third eye enabled him to see the auras everyone has. It opened a window on Tibet and Buddhism that was largely unheard of. But when the publishers asked the few Tibetan scholars in Britain at the time to check its authenticity, the life story of this Lobsang Rampa seemed to be full of inconsistencies. They suspected he'd never even been to Tibet.

Nonetheless, the publishers called Rampa into a meeting. Would Rampa allow them to publish the book as a work of fiction? No, said Rampa and stormed off in a huff. In austere, postwar Britain, Lobsang's book was so different, so out of the nation's frame of reference that the publishers felt it couldn't be anything else but a hit.

Secker & Warburg threw caution to the wind, met Rampa's demands and printed it as a piece of non-fiction. 'Publishers are not the reading police,' says book-trade and publishing expert Alison Baverstock.

> They're not there to say what is true and what isn't true – they're there to find content that other people are interested in reading. This book had a market. It was an accessible, easy-to-read book about Tibetan Buddhism. It gave a lot of

people an introduction into an area of the world they were interested in. I mean, think about it! Everest was climbed in 1953, wasn't it, people were interested in the whole area, but there wasn't a lot of information coming back.

Still, the publishers hedged their bets with a foreword that included what could scarcely be more obviously a disclaimer if it had tried to be: 'The autobiography of a Tibetan lama is a unique record of experience and as such inevitably hard to corroborate.'

The Third Eye was an international bestseller and it was responsible for a huge, and generally positive, spike in Western interest in Buddhism. Lobsang became rich on the royalties. But there was disquiet in the, admittedly still very niche, world of European Tibetan scholars. Among the doubters was Heinrich Harrer. Between 1944 and 1949, he had served as tutor to the fourteenth, and still current, Dalai Lama, the spiritual leader of the Tibetan people. Harrer paid for a private detective called Clifford Burgess, from Liverpool, to do some digging.

Burgess found that Lobsang Rampa was actually a plumber's son called Cyril Henry Hoskin. He was born in the sleepy town of Plympton and worked as a civil servant in Weybridge. He'd never been to Tibet, though he told neighbours in Weybridge that he had once been an instructor in the Chinese Air Force before being invalided out as a result of a parachute accident. There is no evidence to confirm this was true.

In his second, also bestselling, book Rampa explained how he really came to be. As Cyril Hoskin, he had fallen out of a tree while attempting to photograph an owl. As he lay unconscious, his body was taken over by a roaming spirit called Rampa.

Scotland Yard demanded to see Rampa's passport. If he was Tibetan, then he was in the UK without the requisite permissions. Rampa quietly left the UK. Supersleuth Clifford Burgess sprang back into action and tracked Rampa down to a farmhouse in the Republic of Ireland. He was living in a ménage à trois with a female convert and her somewhat nonplussed Eton-educated husband. The papers had a field day and Hoskin/Rampa escaped to Canada to avoid them.

There he continued to write a further 18 bestselling books. One of those was *My Trip to Venus*. This might be Charles Allen's favourite from Lobsang's increasingly strange canon. 'He's picked up by flying saucers and goes to Venus. He goes into another flying saucer, which travels down into the centre of the earth. His last book was dictated to him by his cat – Mrs Fifi Greywhiskers. So he was a man with great imagination!'

Whether or not Cyril genuinely believed he was a Tibetan lama, he stuck to his story until his death in 1981. His books have inspired many by bringing Tibet to the Western world. But there were no tributes from the Tibetan community. The Dalai Lama declared him a fraud and he was disowned by the very people whose lives fascinated him. Nevertheless, of books written about Tibet, *The Third Eye* remains the bestseller. Not bad for a plumber's boy from Devon.

MAKING A FIST OF WOMEN'S RIGHTS

Between 1962 and 1964 actress Honor Blackman's role as leather-suited, judo-throwing, karate-chopping Cathy Gale in *The Avengers* stuck it to the patriarchy by punching through the barriers of male supremacy over women on television. Before Ms. Blackman's TV debut, it was extremely rare to see a woman in a fight on screen, let alone win one without recourse to a gun or heavy blunt instrument. Honor's fighting abilities – channelled through Cathy Gale – caught the eye of producer Cubby Broccoli, then casting for the third – and perhaps most iconic – James Bond film adventure, *Goldfinger*. The role of airplane pilot Pussy Galore was rewritten to accommodate martial arts. Broccoli reasoned, correctly, that British Bond fans would welcome the popular Ms Blackman into the spy franchise, and American audiences would be wowed by the striking, but unknown, ass-kicking dame. ('Dame' in the American sense: Ms. Blackman is a republican and turned down a title in 2002.) The actress became synonymous with martial arts and she wrote a step-by-step guide for women, *Honor Blackman's Book of Self-Defence*, which flew off the shelves.

Honor Blackman, then, was a trailblazer. But she wasn't the pioneer of women in martial arts fighting onscreen – or even off.

That distinction goes to Edith Garrud (1872–1971). This diminutive figure (you'd have been advised not to call her that to her face) literally dragged Britain kicking and screaming into the twentieth century.

Born in Bath, Edith was a physical fitness instructor and martial arts practitioner. In the 1890s this was a highly unusual job for women. But Edith, who was only 1.5 m (4 ft 11 in), spent her life refusing to conform to what was deemed 'normal' (usually by men). She became aware of jujitsu, a Japanese fighting technique, when she took a martial arts class with

Edward Barton Wright, a self-defence expert. Barton Wright had travelled extensively in what was then the almost unheard of country of Japan. For centuries, Japan had closed all of its ports bar one to foreign travellers and traders, but now the nation was slowly opening up. Barton-Wright's writing about what he saw and learned from the Land of the Rising Sun was lapped up back in the UK, where anything and everything Japanese was seen as the height of sophisticated glamour. Gilbert and Sullivan's comic opera *The Mikado* became a huge hit and shops were filled with decorative silk screens and kimono-style dressing gowns. Martial arts, as adapted by Barton-Wright, seemed particularly exotic and also became a British craze.

Edith excelled at the sport and was soon appointed chief instructor at Master Uyenishi's dojo, the School of Japanese Self Defence at 31 Golden Square, London. In 1907, as news reels drew people to the cinema in their thousands, Pathé Films caught the martial arts bug and cast Edith in *Ju-jutsu Downs the Footpads*. The plot involves a purse thief terrorising various London locations, before Edith delivers her own brand of street justice. Until proven otherwise, it's safe to say that Edith was the world's first female martial arts movie star. More significantly, however, was Edith's subsequent role in the women's suffrage movement.

Edith came to the attention of Suffragette leader Emmeline Pankhurst after she gave a demonstration of her fighting skills at a movement meeting. Police violence (and male violence in general) towards the suffragettes was growing in brutality, and Edith was glad to be able to teach the women to defend themselves. Edith believed that jujitsu gave women a method of changing nature. 'Physical force seems the only thing in which women have not demonstrated their equality to men and whilst we are waiting for the evolution which is slowly taking place and bringing about that equality, we might just as well take time by the forelock and use science, otherwise jujitsu,' she wrote in an article for the *Votes for Women* newspaper in 1910.

Edith and jujitsu became synonymous with the suffragette movement. In 1909 the popular fitness magazine *Health & Strength* even coined the term 'Ju-jutsuffragettes', describing the women as 'a new terror for the London Police.'

Within three years she was at the heart of the suffragettes' plans to resist police authority – including training The Bodyguard, an elite group of women formed to protect Pankhurst and prevent her rearrest. When the police next tried to take Pankhurst into custody, The Bodyguard became embroiled in a vicious street fight. Edith was seen to have thrown over her shoulder a policeman weighing 83 kg (13 st). It's worth bearing in mind the fashions of the time. The bare-knuckle suffragettes would have been scrapping in heavy, floor-length dresses and, probably, corsets – plus definitely a hat. But part of the art of jujitsu is being able to disable opponents many times bigger than yourself.

On 1 March 1912, 150 suffragettes met for one of their most audacious protests yet – a renewal of necessary violence in the face of the defeat in the House of Commons of the Conciliation Bill, which would have extended the voting rights of women.

Historian Dr Emelyne Godfrey, who has researched the life of Edith Garrud, explains:

There would be ladies walking around the shops, innocently looking in the windows and then suddenly they would whip out items like a toffee hammer, smash a window and run off. They would put their items under the floorboards, they would get changed for a jujitsu lesson and then the policeman would come knocking on the door. Edith would say, 'This is very, very unchivalrous of you to come in and interrupt a ladies' jujitsu session, we are having a class and I don't know anything about it!'

After the First World War and with votes for women enshrined in law, Edith carried on as a martial arts instructor and lived in Thornhill Square, Islington, until she died aged 99 in 1971.

GREAT SCOTT!

Between the 1950s and 1970s, Peter Scott, hailed in the press as the Human Fly and the King of the Cat Burglars, scaled the sides of stately homes, tunnelled into haute couture boutiques and leapt across the roofs of Mayfair in order to steal the treasures of the rich.

He was born in Belfast in 1931, his real name Peter Craig Gulston. He was a public schoolboy, educated at the Belfast Royal Academy, and therefore cut from a different cloth than the London underworld that toasted him.

Active from his late teens to his sixties, Scott claimed to have relieved the homes of aristocrats, celebrities and the high-end stores they patronised of some £30 million worth of jewellery and luxury goods. 'I realised,' he once said, 'this was my life's work, persecuting the rich and the opulent.'

Scott was so prolific and choosy that some of the upper crust joked it was a snub not to be targeted by him. In crime circles he was lauded for his death-defying ability to climb up to a high window or through a skylight. But to the law-abiding his moral compass definitely pointed south.

Either way, all agreed he had panache. Not for Scott jeans and a balaclava; he wore three-piece suits. He would also wear a new suit for each job, feeling it important to dress in a manner appropriate to the house he was burgling.

Scott used to claim he was nothing more than a dishonest window cleaner. But that didn't stop him having a high opinion of himself. He liked to compare himself with champion jockey Lester Piggott, saying, 'When he threw his leg over a horse you could see the magic. When I threw my leg up a drain pipe, my confederates said they could see the magic, too.'

Police historian and former Met Chief Superintendent Alan Moss was on the beat in central London during Scott's heyday. 'He was an unusual burglar. He was educated and intelligent, so he had an eye for high value people and their goods, and in addition he was athletic and clearly not afraid of heights!' Scott liked to work on his own, but he would have needed a network of blackmarket dealers to exchange the stolen goods for cash – almost certainly at a fraction of their insurance value. 'In the 1950s and '60s the only forensic tool we had for cases like this would be to dust for fingerprints. Scott, of course, would have been wise to that so he always used gloves. The only sure-fire way to get him was to catch him in the act of burglary, collar him in possession of stolen goods or wait for someone to inform on him.'

Alon says that Scott and the particular craft he practised was very much of his time.

Cat burglaries of high profile art and jewellery do still happen, but they're few and far between, crime prevention and detection is just so much more advanced. Cybercrime is the most prevalent nowadays – why bother to go to the efforts and rituals that Peter went to? Burglaries are mainly opportunist now, and sadly tend to be desperate snatches and with perpetrators more inclined to use violence.

Scott wouldn't approve of that. Alan agrees: 'I'm not condoning him, but I'll give Peter this; he saw himself as a gentleman, he viewed his crimes as being as much about the art of planning as the pursuit of profit. There was more skill than putting a brick through a window!'

Perhaps Scott's most notorious job was a theft from the Italian star Sophia Loren. In 1960 Ms. Loren was filming *The Millionairess* with Peter Sellers at Elstree Studios near London. In a newspaper gossip column (to this day known in certain circles as a 'tip' sheet) Scott had read that Loren never travelled without her considerable collection of very expensive jewellery. So he decided to unburden her of it.

Scott researched Loren's movements and, using a stolen press ID card, sauntered into the grounds of the exclusive Edgewarebury Country Club on the pretence of writing a story. Sophia was staying in a luxury cottage known as Norwegian Barn. Peter broke in through a bedroom window and made short shrift of a padlocked tallboy containing approximately £200,000 worth of bling. He could hear Sophia and her husband having dinner in another room, so he muffled the noise of splintering wood by throwing a blanket over him and the drawers.

Audacious and well planned it might have been, but Scott would soon come to regret this particular job. In Sophia Loren he met his match.

Interviewed on TV the day after the burglary the formerly jewel-encrusted Italian star was clearly livid. She uttered a Romany hex aimed at the thief. 'I come from a long line of gypsies. You will have no luck.'

Scott later said that he watched the foreboding message being broadcast that night. As he ate his tea off a tray on his lap, he felt Loren's eyes burning through the screen and deep into his soul.

The crime had the hallmarks of a Scott number, so it wasn't long until the police began asking awkward questions around town. Scott rushed to sell the jewels to a fence. Undoubtedly he got less than their insurance value, but it was enough to buy a brand-new Jaguar car and fund a trip to the glamorous French resort of Cannes. Within days he had lost every penny he'd made in the Palm Beach casino. Sophia never got the jewels back, but her gypsy curse seemed to have paid off.

Scott was undeterred and his lofty crimewave continued – at least, between spells in prison. His targets remained aristos and film stars like Lauren Bacall and Elizabeth Taylor. He also burgled the pied-à-terre of fading star Judy Garland, as she was out appearing in cabaret, but claimed in his memoirs that the *Wizard of Oz* doyenne had no ruby slippers, emeralds or indeed anything of any value hidden in her drawers… so he left empty-handed.

It was age, not the police, which caught up with Peter. So what happens to a cat burglar when he becomes an old dog? Reporter Duncan Campbell, who became friends with Peter in his final years, says:

When you're a living legend it's very hard to change. I think Peter represented a very different, and long-gone era of crime. He was skilled, an artisan thief and never resorted to violence, he was a villain, of the old school. We're strangely nostalgic for that era of crime and he believed and encouraged the romance… At the end, when his knees had gone, it was all he had. He claimed he'd given up crime altogether in 1985, but in 1993 he was caught, red-handed, 'looking after' a Picasso that had been lifted from a Mayfair gallery, and got four years for it.

Surely even Peter could see the game was up? 'He was very near destitute,' says Duncan. 'Every penny he stole he'd lost – mainly through gambling – but he was never self-pitying, more reflective, and on balance I think he felt he'd lived his life to the full. He was slowing down, he tended a rose garden in a London cemetery and you would often see him cycling around fashionable neighbourhoods on a collapsible bike, smiling to himself.' Perhaps dreaming of a drainpipe to shimmy up? 'I wouldn't put it past him,' laughs Duncan.

Peter's last days were spent in a pokey flat on a London council estate in Islington, a short distance, but a far cry, from the Mayfair mansions where the king of the cat burglars had once got his cream. He died in a nursing home aged 82 with nothing but memories to show for his truly remarkable life. Duncan Campbell helped arrange his funeral. 'During the crematorium service I saw a sign on the wall that read: "Warning. Thieves operating in this area. Keep your valuables out of sight." That would have highly amused Peter…"

WEE WILLIE, THE MASTER OF DISGUISE

In the Edinburgh docks district of Leith during the tough interwar years, a policeman's lot was seldom a happy one. You had to be as hard as the villains you were chasing, and the number one requirement for being a copper was an imposing physicality. But an exception was made for one pint-sized wannabe. He proved to have so much guile he would become a giant of the force.

At 1.67 m (5 ft 6 in), William Merrilees was 10 cm (4 in) below the then regulation height for police en. But he turned his lack of stature to his advantage: becoming a master of disguise, he dressed as an old lady, a porter and even a baby in order to nab criminals.

During an event-packed career he was shot at and slashed at while busting safecrackers and nabbing gangsters. He retired as a Chief Constable, OBE, to write his memoirs, *The Short Arm of the Law*, an autobiography that today feels more Hollywood than Holyrood.

Some had their doubts about some of his stories, but what is known to be true is that William Merrilees was born in poverty in Leith in 1898. He left school at 13 for the ropeworks of the famous shipyards. Just months into the job, his sleeve caught in a winding mechanism and he lost four of the fingers on his left hand.

Refusing to be defined by his disability, the now 14-year-old Willie returned to the docks and mastered a two-handed drill. But more remarkable still were the eight separate times he dived into the icy waters of the Leith to save the lives of dockworkers who'd fallen in.

Acclaimed crime novelist Tony Black says Willie's heroism led to a story you just couldn't make up.

> Apparently he had rescued so many people that the Provost
> – or the mayor, as he would be known down south – said to
> him at the time, 'What can we do for you?' He replied that
> he'd like to be a policeman and of course the Provost said,
> 'I think they'd probably laugh at that suggestion, Willie, but
> I tell you what, I'll give it a go.'

Amazingly, a dispensation was made and Willie was allowed to join the force. But it was a disappointing start to his career, says Tony.

> Initially Willie was parked behind a desk, but one day they
> were short-staffed, so he was asked to show a wanted mug-
> shot around town. Fate jumped in because one of the first
> people he showed it to was the villain himself, who hared
> off up the street. Willie chased him, cuffed him and won his
> first collar. From there on nothing could stop him.

Part Batman, part Jimmy Krankie (the fictitious Scottish TV scallywag), Willy had a flair for the theatrical, which meant that he surprised the denizens of the underworld in a variety of unexpected get-ups. He once dressed as a railway porter and arrested a suspected German spy who was just about to board a train from the platform of Edinburgh's Waverly station; it transpired the man was armed with a Mauser pistol and had a radio transmitter concealed in his suitcase. On another occasion he dragged up as a little old lady in order to foil a bag-snatching gang. But his masterpiece, surely, was the time he dressed as a baby – complete with a bonnet – and lay in wait in a specially adapted pram to leap out at a pervert who had been pestering nannies in an Edinburgh park.

Willie soon became nationally famous as 'the pocket-sized detective with the battleship reputation'. Unconventional but charismatic, Wee Willie raised the eyebrows of his superiors but won the respect of the officers he rose through the ranks to lead. Combined with his charity work, he would be honoured with the ultimate TV accolade – an episode of *This Is Your Life* when Eamonn Andrews threw the Big Red Book at him.

A hard nut he might have been, but Chief Constable Merrilee's had a soft centre, too, according to his granddaughter Margaret:

He was very theatrical. I used to love all the stories about him dressing up, he wasn't afraid to act the fool if it meant a collar. People say he was formidable, but I remember him as a very sweet, kind man. He raised so much for different charities, even for the families of the men he arrested. He knew what poverty was like and he knew what it was like to struggle with life, so he always tried to give people a second chance.

TWO BOBBIES

Willie has a close connection to another Edinburgh legend. In the late nineteenth century Greyfriars Bobby was a wee Skye Terrier that stood guard over the grave of his late master John Gray, in Edinburgh's Greyfriars Kirkyard, for 14 years – until his own death in 1872.

Gray had been a nightwatchman in the Edinburgh Police Force and when he succumbed to tuberculosis in 1858, the loyal dog refused to leave his master's grave.

Presumably the dog was just called Bobby prior to Gray's demise, but either way it's a charming – and true – story that became the basis of a popular novel, *Greyfriars Bobby* by American writer Eleanor Atkinson in 1912. It is not known whether Atkinson ever visited Edinburgh herself or had read about the famous canine in articles that had been printed in the *New York Times* and *Our Animal Friends*. Either way, the author's imagination had been captured by the fiercely loyal dog.

Fifty years later, the book was optioned by Walt Disney for a film of the same name, which was shot on location in Edinburgh and featured a great performance by a cute Skye Terrier called Wee Bobby. Prior to the production, Willie Merrilees had met Walt Disney on a trip to America; the two became friends, so Uncle Walt asked Willie to scout the film's locations. As a thank you, Disney gave Wee Bobby to Willie and the two became inseparable; Wee Bobby even had the honour of being joint best man at Merrilees' wedding.

ACKNOWLEDGEMENTS

Michael Armit
Sandy Smith
Seb lllis
Simon Shaw
Tessa Finch
Owen Gay
Laura Marshall
Harry Marshall
Andie Clare
Lucy Middelboe
Stephen McQuillan
Phoebe Sinclair
Cris Warren
Duncan Haskell
Jack Miller
Dan Phillips
Dominic Weston
Asad Kara
James Dundas
Julian Alexander

Huge thanks to all the Execs, Directors, Researchers, Production Coordinators, Camera Operators, Editors (online and off), Runners and work experience students who worked on Icon Films' One Show desk over the past decade. As well as the wider Icon Films staff who, in numerous different ways, all helped to make the One Show short films a reality - even roping in their friends, family, neighbours, casual acquaintances and pets when necessary. There are too many of you to name individually but you did an amazing job and you all share the blame for this book!

ACKNOWLEDGEMENTS